Praise for *How Can My Kid Succeed in School?*

"With his book, *How Can My Kid Succeed in School?*, Craig Pohlman reminds all of us—especially parents and teachers—that effective teaching cannot occur unless we better understand learning. By examining the 'goodness of fit' between student learning profiles and the curriculum taught in school, Pohlman offers practical educational strategies and approaches that will ensure academic success for all kids."

—*Michael E. Spagna, dean, Michael D. Eisner College of Education, California State University, Northridge*

"This is an important book . . . Dr. Pohlman has provided a systematic and easy-to-follow approach that parents and teachers can use to help students find greater success in school."

—*Elizabeth Briere, M.D., FAAP, pediatrician and executive director, Success in Mind*

"Parents and teachers alike will find Dr. Pohlman's book enlightening, reassuring, and incredibly helpful in guiding struggling learners towards success in school. His book is full of clear examples and strategies, presented in language all will understand. With *How Can My Kid Succeed in School?*, readers will be able to help children and adolescents find the success they deserve."

—*Tim Barrier, head of school, Stanley British Primary School, Denver, Colorado*

JOSSEY-BASS TEACHER

Jossey-Bass Teacher provides educators and parents with practical knowledge and tools to create a positive and lifelong impact on student learning. We offer classroom-tested and research-based teaching resources for a variety of grade levels and subject areas. Whether you are a parent, teacher, or another professional working with children in grades K–12, we want to help you make every learning experience successful.

From ready-to-use learning activities to the latest teaching framework, our value-packed books provide insightful, practical, and comprehensive materials on the topics that matter most. We hope to become your trusted source for the best ideas from the most experienced and respected experts in the field.

How Can My Kid Succeed in School?

WHAT PARENTS AND TEACHERS CAN DO TO
CONQUER LEARNING PROBLEMS

Craig Pohlman

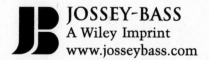
JOSSEY-BASS
A Wiley Imprint
www.josseybass.com

Published by Jossey-Bass
A Wiley Imprint
989 Market Street, San Francisco, CA 94103-1741—www.josseybass.com

Jossey-Bass books and products are available through most bookstores. To contact Jossey-Bass directly call our Customer Care Department within the U.S. at 800-956-7739, outside the U.S. at 317-572-3986, or fax 317-572-4002.

Jossey-Bass also publishes its books in a variety of electronic formats. Some content that appears in print may not be available in electronic books.

Library of Congress Cataloging-in-Publication Data has been applied for.

ISBN 978-047-0-38376-6

Printed in the United States of America
FIRST EDITION
PB Printing   10 9 8 7 6 5 4 3 2 1

THE AUTHOR

Craig Pohlman directs learning assessment and consultation services at Southeast Psych in Charlotte, NC. A licensed psychologist and nationally certified school psychologist, he began his career teaching science to elementary and middle school students in New York City. He later earned his doctorate in school psychology at the University of North Carolina at Chapel Hill (UNC-CH), where he trained at The Clinical Center of the Student of Development and Learning, University of North Carolina School of Medicine (CDL). After an internship in the Dallas Public Schools, he returned to the CDL for a post-doctoral fellowship. He later earned appointments at UNC-CH as Clinical Assistant Professor in the school psychology program and as Clinical Scientist at the CDL. As Senior Clinical Scholar at All Kinds of Minds, he helped develop the core knowledge for products, tools, and services.

Dr. Pohlman has conducted or supervised thousands of assessments of struggling learners and has trained thousands of professionals on assessment techniques. He also has designed numerous techniques and tools to help others integrate a neurodevelopmental assessment approach into their work with students. His previous book, *Revealing Minds,* is a hands-on guide for professionals who assess students facing learning challenges.

About Southeast Psych

The mission of Southeast Psych (www.southeastpsych.com) is to put psychology into the hands of as many people as possible to enhance their lives. Based in Charlotte, NC, Southeast Psych provides a range of mental health services across the life span, including assessment, therapy, and professional training. The clinicians of Southeast Psych have authored numerous books and have been featured nationally in *USA Today, Newsweek,* NPR, NBC News, and in dozens of newspapers around the country.

About All Kinds of Minds

All Kinds of Minds (www.allkindsofminds.org) is a not-for-profit organization that translates the latest research from neuroscience and other disciplines on how children learn—and vary in their learning—into a powerful framework that educators can use in the classroom. Their professional development courses offer both breakthrough ideas and practical solutions for educators to unlock the potential of all children, including those who learn differently.

For Jennifer—my fellow adventurer

CONTENTS

PART TWO
CONQUERING LEARNING PROBLEMS AT SCHOOL
89

PART THREE
WHEN MORE HELP IS NEEDED
149

PREFACE

I've been in the education and learning field for two decades. I started my career as an educator—a classroom teacher and tutor—and then became a psychologist. Along the way I've met thousands of kids, parents, educators, and clinicians. I'd like to think that I've learned quite a bit from my experiences with all of those people, but nothing has had a more significant effect on me, professionally and personally, than becoming a father.

Before the birth of my first son I'd interacted with many, many parents fraught with worry and frustrated about their children's learning struggles. I used my clinical training and professional experience to support them as best I could. As a parent, though, I could finally, truly empathize with those who were in anguish because their children were suffering. That insight was the main reason I wrote this book. I wanted to draw from my perspectives as a psychologist, former teacher, and father to create a resource to help parents whose children are having a tough time with school. In a sense, this book's organization reflects my three perspectives: Part One is a set of tools for parents, Part Two is a toolbox for educators, and Part Three is a road map for parents and teachers for collaborating with clinicians.

Lots of books on learning have been written for parents and teachers. This book takes a unique leap of faith: that if parents and teachers are equipped with the knowledge of what to look for, they can actually identify many of the brain factors underlying learning problems. Put simply, parents and teachers can uncover a great deal about students' strengths and weaknesses.

I hope this book opens new opportunities for my fellow clinicians—opportunities to work with parents and educators who have devoted time and energy to thinking about students, to get detailed observations from home and school, and to be asked good referral questions to frame their assessments. In this regard I acknowledge Dr. Jerome Groopman, whose tremendous book *How Doctors Think* made me contemplate the parent-clinician partnership and how parents can positively affect the thought processes of clinicians.

Parents and teachers are in a unique position to observe students and, with a little guidance, can do a lot of deep thinking about specific strengths and weaknesses. If all the answers can't be found at home or in the classroom, clinicians can add their expertise to the mix. After all, everyone who works with kids—parents, teachers, clinicians—is in this together.

INTRODUCTION

BRADY IS A SECOND GRADER WHO'S HAVING A VERY HARD TIME LEARNING to read and spell. He's great at art, enthusiastically listens to stories, and absorbs information he hears (he loves learning about reptiles). He is picking up math skills with no trouble and is a natural when collaborating with peers. Both adults and kids really enjoy being around him, but his reading troubles are starting to deflate him. In first grade he dashed out the door every morning to get to school. Now he asks if he has to go, and longs for weekends and vacations.

Cetera is Brady's classmate. She also struggles with reading and spelling. Although not quite so social as Brady, she belongs to a very close threesome of friends. She loves sports, especially soccer and basketball. Cetera also is starting to have some trouble with math. Like Brady, she picks up information very easily when listening, though sometimes she has a hard time making connections with her prior knowledge. Lately she's been complaining to her mother about how hard school is for her.

How can Brady's and Cetera's learning problems be conquered? How can their parents and teachers get them to enjoy school again? Figuring out what is causing their reading challenges is the first step. The good news is that their parents and teachers can gather lots of information, analyze it, and then select targeted learning strategies, but they have to know what to look for and how to make sense of what they find. This book helps with both.

Like all students, Brady and Cetera leave plenty of clues about their learning. For example, Brady has a hard time coming up with rhyming words. When he reads aloud he drops out word sounds (such as reading *block* as *bok*) and inserts letters that shouldn't be there when he spells (such as spelling *candy* as *canku*). Cetera struggles with memory for several types of information, such as math facts and prior knowledge.

Brady's clues add up to the conclusion that word sounds are very confusing to him. He doesn't clearly process small sounds like /f/ in *leaf*, which means he has a hard time connecting sounds with letters (like /f/ with *f* or *ph* or even *gh*, as in *cough*). In contrast, Cetera processes small word sounds just fine (for instance, she can rhyme and move sounds around to change words). As it turns out, she has a hard time remembering which sounds go with which letters.

By the way, both Brady and Cetera would probably meet criteria for a learning disability (or more specifically, a reading disability or dyslexia), but labeling them wouldn't do much good. That would be akin to claiming that a child with stomach pain has something like Abdomen Soreness Disorder—a label that is pretty useless when it comes to a treatment. Labels tend to oversimplify students by not capturing unique characteristics, such as the differences between Brady and Cetera. Also, labels don't convey strengths and interests, such as Brady's affinity for reptiles or Cetera's listening comprehension.

If a child complained of stomach pain, you'd go groping in the dark for a cure if you didn't know the cause. Could it be a virus? How about acid reflux? Did he eat something that had spoiled? Is the pain a symptom of stress or worry?

Brady and Cetera are experiencing unique challenges. Understanding the specifics of those challenges helps identify what they need in order to be more successful readers. For Brady, the key is to bolster his capacity to process word sounds. Cetera, on the other hand, needs drill in matching sounds to letters in order to solidify this information in her memory banks. By working in these specific areas, they can make strides in their reading and feel successful again.

Why Understanding a Profile Is So Important

As Brady and Cetera show, knowing why a student is having a hard time with an academic skill, such as reading, paves the way to choices that have the best chance of helping. But understanding a learner is critical for many other reasons as well. For example, identifying a student's strengths is just as important as uncovering weaknesses. For so many struggling learners, only shortcomings get discussed or addressed. But every student has strengths or talents and deserves to have them highlighted and celebrated. A student who has been coming up short academically will especially benefit from hearing about the things he does well.

Sometimes strengths aren't readily apparent and have to be discovered by parents and teachers who are willing to look closely for them.

Having a deep understanding of a kid's strengths and weaknesses also helps adults move toward a more positive mindset. Negative thinking has a way of creeping in when working with a challenging student. *If only he were motivated to try harder! The kid is just lazy! When she decides to do it, she can do it! He's never going to get it! She may never be successful! He's so frustrating!* If you know the specific reasons that a student (such as Brady) is struggling (because his brain doesn't reliably process small word sounds), then empathizing is easier. After all, it's not Brady's fault his mind is wired a certain way. In fact, it's nobody's fault, it's just a reality. What's more, identifying a child's strengths can also help others gain a fresh perspective on him. *I never realized how good he was at that!*

Learning problems are seldom cured. Instead, they need to be managed over the long haul—sometimes for years, maybe even for a lifetime. For a parent, helping a child with a learning problem is a long and challenging journey fraught with disappointments and victories, heartbreaks and breakthroughs, downturns and turning points. A parent makes thousands of decisions over the course of a child's academic career, ranging from how to help get a book report done to picking the right school. Parents need a set of charts to navigate these hazard-filled waters. This is a guidebook for parents of students with learning problems, to help them help their struggling children.

The foundational ideas of this book draw from the groundbreaking work of renowned pediatrician and learning expert Mel Levine. His thinking is described in books such as *A Mind at a Time*.

Obviously teachers also are critical to the educational journey of a student. Like parents, teachers need to understand the specific reasons for a struggling student's learning breakdowns in order to make instructional decisions. In some important ways, Brady and Cetera need to be taught differently so they can improve their reading skills. Teachers are in a position to learn so much about a student's profile of strengths and weaknesses, because of the numerous opportunities they have for observation and access to work samples.

Teachers also have tremendous power to tap into the strengths and interests of their students. All kids, but especially those who are struggling, need chances to explore the things they do well. To be sure, all of the current emphasis on standards and preparation for group tests makes discovering and nurturing affinities and talents harder than ever. But looking at kids in terms of their profiles, and then tapping into those strengths and weaknesses, should be folded into the daily work in the classroom and not an added burden. Figuring out what is going on with Brady and Cetera, for example, should happen naturally and not during overtime.

Thinking "Neurodevelopmentally"

Knowing a student's neurodevelopmental strengths and weaknesses is so important for helping them. But what does *neurodevelopmental* mean, anyway? *Neuro-* is a prefix that refers to brain functioning. *Developmental*, obviously, is what we all know to be true—that children change over time. So *neurodevelopmental* refers to brain functioning that changes over time. Babies enter the world with a set of genes that are the starting points for countless characteristics and abilities that unfold over the lifespan. One way to think about this is that we inherit from the gene pool ranges for traits and abilities rather than specific amounts. For example, very tall parents will likely pass on to a child the genes for a height range that is higher than for most other kids (say, six feet, six inches to six feet, eleven inches, though there's actually no way to quantify this), but where their child will end up in that range (closer to six feet, six inches, or to six feet, eleven inches) depends on life experience. Does he eat a nutritious diet with plenty of calcium? Did she contract any illnesses that might stunt growth?

Two terms that get used a lot in developmental psychology are *nature* and *nurture*. *Nature* refers to the range for an inherited ability, *nurture* refers to what happens over time to move that ability up or down in that range. Nature and nurture play a huge role in learning. For example, Brady probably was born with a range for the processing of word sounds that was a bit lower relative to other students' ranges. Over time, though, his life experiences may not have provided all the practice his brain needed to maximize what he could do with word sounds. Cetera's capacity for memory unfolded in the same way, subject to the forces of nature and nurture.

> Focusing on the here and now is so critical that if you sense yourself dwelling on past events, repeat a mantra of some kind. Use a phrase like "no day but today," "water under the bridge," or "we are where we are."

When we are trying to understand and help a struggling learner, the focus needs to be on the here and now. Worrying about genes or early life experiences that may have brought about current learning challenges is rarely helpful; but recognizing the joint role of nature and nurture can be liberating because it can give hope that with the right instruction and strategies, nurture can work on your side—to push a set of abilities toward the upper range that nature programmed. Evidence exists that brain structure can be altered as a result of positive educational experiences. The term for such change is *plasticity*, which captures the idea that the brain is a bit like a malleable plastic. So we can improve Brady's processing of word sounds and Cetera's memory for sound-symbol pairs; it will require work and take some time, but it can be done.

Weaknesses aren't the only things that can be changed by life experience. A neurodevelopmental strength is also a brain-based ability that changes over time but is operating very well for a kid, maybe just as it should for his age. Clues can reveal a student's neurodevelopmental strengths. Brady's talent with art is a clue that he has good visual abilities, or *spatial ordering*. The fact that he can absorb so much information when listening is a tip-off that he has strong *receptive language*, or the capacity to interpret words, sentences, and passages. In addition, given how easily he collaborates with others, it's not surprising that he has terrific social skills.

> A neurodevelopmental weakness is not a complete lack of ability but rather an unreliable or shaky ability (like a radio with fuzzy reception). Brady can process many word sounds and Cetera can remember some sound-symbol pairs. They just can't always count on these respective abilities when they need them.

A neurodevelopmental profile is a set of neurodevelopmental strengths and weaknesses. Every human brain has both strengths and weaknesses, so every person has a profile. When helping a struggling learner, uncovering the profile is the critical first step.

The profile helps navigate decisions about the best strategies and instruction. The profile highlights the student's strengths, some of which may never have been noticed before someone took a closer look. Profiles, not labels and diagnostic categories, are what we all should be using to describe learners. Calling Brady and Cetera dyslexic just tells us they have a hard time reading. A diagnostic label like *learning disability* or *reading disorder* tells us nothing about their strengths and the reasons for their struggles.

I often drop the term *neurodevelopmental* and use only *strength* (for *neurodevelopmental strength*), *weakness* (for *neurodevelopmental weakness*), and *profile* (for *neurodevelopmental profile*).

One other point about thinking neurodevelopmentally: neurodevelopmental abilities or functions are numerous, and each has a range in terms of how well it operates for a person. Consequently, an infinite number of possible neurodevelopmental profiles exists. In other words, every kid (really, every human being) has a unique profile, a unique mind. This variation is natural and necessary for a vibrant world. We need people who can see and do things differently from others. In adulthood, companies and organizations actively seek different skill sets so that everything can get accomplished. We just need for schools to be better equipped to handle variation in learning styles.

All Kinds of Minds (www.allkindsofminds.org) is a non-profit institute for the understanding of differences in learning. It offers various products, tools, and services for those who work with struggling students.

How This Book Is Organized

The chapters of this book are organized into three parts, each relating to a progressive stage in developing an understanding of a student's profile. Part One is about what can be done at home and is written primarily with parents in mind, although educators will also find this material useful in rounding out their knowledge of learning and in advising their students' parents on what to look for at home. Part Two describes what can be done at school and is written primarily for educators; it will also give parents a better understanding of the academic experience and equip them to discuss learning issues with teachers. To help a struggling learner, parent-teacher collaboration is a must.

Parts One and Two each contain two chapters, one devoted to gathering and interpreting information in order to reveal a student's profile (that is, to knowing what clues to look for and how to make sense of them), the other focused on using the student's learning profile to make good choices about strategies and teaching approaches. The chapters on gathering and interpreting information (One and Three) are organized by setting (such as homework time) or the opportunity to find clues (such as reviewing work samples). Both chapters present clues and explain the learning strengths and weaknesses that could be behind them. Once you have taken the available clues and translated them into neurodevelopmental possibilities, you'll be ready for the chapters on strategies and teaching approaches (Two and Four).

Some profiles contain elements that are more difficult to uncover than other elements, and some learning problems are so challenging that parents and teachers need additional support. Part Three is about getting what you need from professional expertise. This section of the book prepares parents especially, but also educators, to be effective consumers of clinical services—how to find the right clinician, how to set the stage for a productive assessment, how to get the most out of the assessment so that the student can be more successful.

Parents and educators will learn a lot from this book by reading it all the way through, but it is designed also to be a reference or guidebook so that readers can return to specific sections when the need arises. Several tables and figures are provided to present information clearly and to be used for quick reference; several appendixes can be consulted for additional information. Most chapters begin with a set of "starting pointers" that are tips for having the right mindset when working with a struggling learner. The "bottom line" ideas found at the end of several chapters are also intended to frame thinking. Hopefully your copy will end up getting dog-eared, marked up, and stuffed with bookmarks.

So, let's get started. First we'll head into the home and family environment to describe the various clues there that can reveal a learner's strengths and weaknesses.

Conquering Learning Problems at Home

"The thing about learning problems is that there is no magic cure. If I'm not my son's advocate, no one will be. As his advocate, I have to sift through feedback and resources to come up with the best strategies to help him. But the most important thing has been communicating with him so that he understands his challenges in a concrete way. That's made us partners in this, and it's given him a sense that things aren't so bad, that there's hope."

—PARENT

"My daughter was empowered by being able to name her challenge with decoding and spelling as a weakness with letter patterns as opposed to her ability to think deeply about what she reads. She could then put her finger on a specific issue that we could work on rather than think of herself as faulty in some overall way. Also, it was great for her to realize how well she can share her insightful thoughts with her expressive language."

—PARENT

1

Looking for Clues at Home

AN EDUCATION IS NOT CONFINED BY SCHOOL WALLS. SO MUCH LEARNING happens at home, from memorizing multiplication tables to reviewing spelling words to writing book reports to studying for biology exams. So a great deal can be learned about learning at home. Parents can discover a lot about their child's profile as long as they know what to look for.

This chapter focuses on what parents can observe about learning and is structured around specific settings and opportunities:

- *Homework time.* For many families, this time can be difficult for everyone as kids struggle to get through academic work that pushes against their learning weaknesses. The good news is that because students are grappling with such tasks, homework provides numerous windows into a child's profile.
- *Review of work samples.* A collection of student work (such as writing or math) is a treasure trove of clues as long as you know how to sift them out.
- *Free time.* What a kid does at play, at meal time, during conversations, and while completing (or trying to complete) chores around the house can all provide tip-offs about learning strengths and weaknesses.

- We'll also take a look at the issue of *organization*, not just because so many parents are concerned about how their child organizes his work and materials, but also because organization can be a touchstone for a kid's profile.

Most of the chapter's sections include a table listing clues that can be gathered, along with possible connections with a child's learning profile. These tables can serve as quick references for interpreting what you are seeing. Along the way we'll meet more kids like Brady and Cetera, students whose particular learning profiles make aspects of school really challenging. The chapter concludes with the "bottom line," a few parting thoughts related to learning about your child's learning. We'll kick off with some "starting pointers," or initial thoughts to help you frame your thinking during this journey of revealing your child's strengths and weaknesses.

Starting Pointers

1. *Always keep your eyes open* to potential clues about your child's learning. Even when a kid is not doing schoolwork, he may be doing or saying something that can be a window into a strength or weakness.

2. *At the outset, focus just on gathering clues.* Spend time simply observing (or listening, or reviewing work), even though you may be tempted to try to figure out what's happening. This urge is natural and expected, because you desperately want to help your child, but you'll gather more and better clues if your mind is relatively free of biases. Once you have pulled together different kinds of information from various settings, you can start trying to make sense of it (the next section describes the thought process for interpreting clues). You can use the Profile Worksheet (provided in Appendix One) to organize your clues. This worksheet

includes a column for *trouble signs* and another for *positive signs.* The information offered in this chapter will help you place clues in the proper rows for the different neurodevelopmental functions. After placing several clues on the worksheet, you should begin to see patterns emerge, such as difficulties with attention or strengths with memory.

3. *Find a basis for comparison.* All students' skills and abilities progress through time (that's the nature of development), so knowing approximately where a student is on a continuum, using other kids as anchor points, is important. For example, you might observe that your second grader prints with a heavy hand (which can be a tip-off about something called *graphomotor function,* the coordination of movements necessary for controlling a pencil), but you'll need to have a sense of how other second graders handle a pencil in order to say whether the heavy printing is out of the ordinary. Sources of comparison include older siblings (reflect back on how they handled similar tasks), friends, classmates, and teachers. *You don't need to study standards and grade-level expectations to do this!* You just need to have some general markers for reality checks.

4. *Take a good look at contrasts in performance.* One of the most useful kinds of clues you can find is a difference between two of a kid's skills or abilities, because such a difference often reveals a strength on one hand and a weakness on the other. For instance, Nabia is a ninth grader who is having a terrible time with tests. A review of her errors shows that she has particular trouble on open-ended and fill-in-the-blank questions, which require her to pull information out of her memory banks with little help. In contrast, she is far more successful with recognition questions (such as multiple choice), which provide a prompt or cue. This is an important difference to note for Nabia, because it is probably telling us that she can store information in her

long-term memory (which is why she can answer recognition questions) but struggles with retrieving it (which is why free-recall questions are pitfalls for her). Later I point out other types of contrasts to look for and discuss what they might mean.

5. *Make extra effort to look for strengths,* because slipping into the trap of focusing on weaknesses is so easy. Bear in mind that a strength isn't always an off-the-charts talent. Sometimes highlighting a neurodevelopmental function that is operating just as it should is important; for a student who has had a lot of bad experiences with school, hearing that something is working OK may be very good news. Also, some strengths are relative to a student's weaknesses. Nabia's overall long-term memory, for example, might be weak relative to that of other ninth graders, but she should probably know that her ability to store information is a strength relative to her ability to retrieve it.

6. *By "peeking behind" weaknesses, you may uncover strengths.* This book describes many things to look for that will allow you to go below the surface of a learning problem. Many times an unknown asset emerges that had been blanketed by a weakness. Felix is another ninth grader whose parents worry about his study skills. Like Nabia, Felix is able to store material in his long-term memory; the catch is that his attention gets in the way. His attention *processing control* is unreliable, meaning that he glosses over details and is easily distracted; but when he locks onto material, he can remember it very well.

Deciphering the Clues

Before we get into the different clues about learning that you can find at home, let's preview how you'll make sense of them.

Again, you should devote time just to gathering information and not jump to conclusions. Once you've taken a look at your child in different settings and doing various kinds of work, think of the deciphering process as like sorting cards. You'll have a bunch of clues, each of which is like a card. In fact, some people might find it helpful to write each piece of information on an index card and then lay them out on a table in categories representing neurodevelopmental areas.

> Chapters One and Three are about translating clues (such as observations made during homework time) into neurodevelopmental areas (such as attention and memory). Chapters Two and Four describe strategies for addressing those neurodevelopmental areas.

The process is about taking the information you've gathered and organizing it into a framework that allows you to look at patterns. Figure 1.1. lists (on the left side) a lot of observations that were made about a kid's writing that were then sorted into three neurodevelopmental areas (on the right side). Once the sorting process is complete, the evidence of a child's strengths and weaknesses is laid out. The following sections contain tables that display possible connections between clues. These tables (as well as the Atlas of Neurodevelopmental Terms provided in Appendix Three) will help you sort your cards, so to speak.

Making Discoveries During Homework Time

Many parents of struggling students describe homework time as a challenging, frustrating experience for the entire family: the kid is forced to do work he has a very hard time with (rather than playing or doing more enjoyable things), the parent feels like a

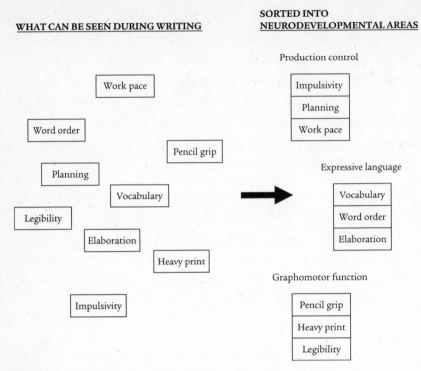

Figure 1.1 *Interpreting Information About Learning*

drill sergeant, siblings may be caught in the crossfire, and everyone feels like their worst qualities are exposed. In the face of these uphill battles, being an objective observer of clues is critical. Many things can be done to make homework time more productive and calm, but the first step is to get a handle on the underlying problems. (The next chapter includes strategies for homework time based on the neurodevelopmental functions that might be involved.)

The good news is that homework is a great opportunity to find clues about learning, not only because the student is grappling with academic tasks but also because homework time has some key differences from the classroom setting: the student is alone, he doesn't have the support of a teacher readily available, and the time may be more concentrated on work (whereas classroom time is consumed by transitions, giving instructions, cleaning up materials, and so on). Here we'll cover both what to watch for during homework time and clues you can pick up on by listening.

In the course of describing the various clues you can discover at home, I mention several functions (in *italics*) that are described in more detail in the Atlas of Neurodevelopmental Terms.

Handling a Pencil

You can start making important observations about your child's profile the moment he picks up a pencil. For a lot of students, handwriting is a huge barrier to academic productivity. Pencil control, legibility, hand fatigue, and handwriting speed can all prevent good ideas and knowledge from making it onto the paper. The way your child holds a pencil is the first clue to graphomotor function. The best way to hold a pencil is with what is called a *tripod grip*, formed by the thumb and middle fingers (which make most of the movements to form letters) and the forefinger (which regulates pressure against the paper), with the pencil at about a forty-five-degree angle to the writing surface.

Pencil grips can go awry in a lot of ways, such as wrapping the thumb around the forefinger and middle finger, so that the forefinger is not stabilizing the pencil, or excessively hooking the wrist. Figure 1.2 shows photographs of pencil grips, including a tripod grip and three troublesome grips. When we write, the nerves in the hand and wrist send signals back to the brain about where the pencil is in the letter formation process. If these signals are weak or get crossed, then relying heavily on sight to

Tripod grip (ideal). Thumb and middle finger control most of the pencil movement at their middle joints, and the forefinger regulates pressure. The pencil is at about a 45-degree angle to the writing surface.

Thumb overwrap. Thumb is wrapped around the joints of the forefinger and middle finger, making it hard to move them. As a result, the pencil must be moved mostly with the wrist; little movements are harder, but the wrist gives feedback on pencil position.

Forefinger out of action. Forefinger doesn't stabilize the pencil as it should. The pencil is perpendicular to the writing surface. As a result, too many joints are needed to move the pencil.

Hooked wrist. Wrist is excessively hooked and the pencil is held very tightly (with the end of the forefinger very flexed). The hand may stiffen and tire quickly when writing.

Figure 1.2 *Handwriting Grips*

photography by Patti Donnelly

monitor the pencil tip may be necessary. So if your child really needs to watch what the tip of his pencil is doing, that could be a trouble sign. Later in this chapter we'll cover a set of clues related to what handwritten work looks like.

Planning and Organizing

How a kid goes about doing his homework can be very revealing. A lot of parents are dismayed when their child seems to leap right into tasks without first contemplating the best course of action. Courtney, a sixth grader, fits this bill. Her mother describes her as a "bull in a china shop" when it comes to homework (and incidentally, most other times when a methodical approach is called for as well). When Courtney gets to a math word problem, she seems to start scribbling calculations before she even finishes reading it. Sometimes she answers almost all of the questions in social studies assignments before realizing that the directions wanted her to do something else. But above all, her writing is a disaster. The notion of starting with an outline is totally alien to Courtney, who would much rather just get to writing; as a result, many of her great ideas never make it to the page or get hidden in a disorganized stream of sentences.

This book describes attention in a way that is new to many people. Rather than thinking of attention as part of a diagnosis (namely attention deficit hyperactivity disorder), it can be more useful to view it as a set of brain functions (production control, processing control, and mental energy), each of which oversees different aspects of working and thinking. This model of attention was developed by Dr. Mel Levine.

Courtney has a weakness in an aspect of her attention called *production control*, which is like the brain's dashboard; her mind doesn't have a reliable speedometer, meaning that she jumps into tasks too quickly, without first coming up with good plans. Dashboards also provide many signals (such as a low-fuel light and a door-ajar signal) to let you know how well things are working, but Courtney's production control doesn't monitor her work very effectively. Her mother gets exasperated by all of the "careless" mistakes she makes in her homework. For example, she might miscalculate in math or misspell a word, but when prompted to take a second look, she readily finds these kinds of errors and fixes them.

Staying on Task

Tate is a fourth grader and his dad says that homework "takes *forever* to get done." The reason? Tate is very susceptible to distractions and daydreaming due to his attention processing control. His dad frequently reels him back in with little reminders like "Stick with it, Tate" or "Come on back, dude!" Getting homework done in a reasonable amount of time usually requires great effort to stay focused on the task at hand.

Everyone, including adults, experiences difficulty with concentration from time to time. Even if you're working in a place with few distracting sights and sounds, your thoughts may wander like Tate's. For some people, processing control does not do a sufficient job of resisting "mind trips" and avoiding distractions. If given a choice between finishing homework and spending time on recreational activities, most kids would choose the latter; but kids with weak processing control are pulled even more strongly than other kids toward fun stuff and away from work.

A kid can have a hard time staying on task for reasons other than weak attention, however. *Active working memory* is what we use to mentally juggle or manipulate information.

Reverse the sequence of digits in your phone number without using a pencil and paper. You've just used your active working memory.

Monika frequently gets lost in the middle of homework tasks. As a seventh grader, much of her work involves multiple steps (such as when solving a math problem) or numerous components that have to be attended to simultaneously (such as all the aspects of writing a book report). In other words, she has to handle a lot of moving parts, and her parents see her losing track of a lot of them. So she may get lost in the middle of a math computation and complain that she is confused about what to do next.

Keeping the Energy Up

Thinking, like physical activity, requires energy. Homework can really tap into a kid's mental fuel tank, which may be drained after a long day of school. So, showing a little "brain drain" during homework is natural; but a pattern of excessive fatigue, night in and night out, may signal problems with *mental energy*, a third aspect of attention. The most taxing academic work is writing, because it requires so many types of thinking (such as vocabulary, spelling, and idea generation) for a sustained period. Therefore, a good time to observe how well a kid's mental energy is holding up is during written work. Also, a kid who is extremely drawn to fun activities, which aren't nearly as draining as homework, may have unreliable mental energy.

Information Literacy

Most parents would agree that their child's education experience is much different than their own was. One of the biggest differences is how technology is now folded into academics. Practically every classroom and most homes have at least one computer. Students use computers for all types of school activities, including word processing their writing, building slide show presentations, and playing learning games (such as for math facts or phonics). With most computers connected to the Internet, students have the capacity to access an incredible volume and variety of content. *Information literacy*, or the skills used to access (with search engines) and evaluate digital information, has emerged as an academic skill that is as important as the traditional skill areas of reading, writing, and mathematics.

Information literacy can be undermined by neurodevelopmental weaknesses just like the traditional skills can. Closely watching how a kid engages with digital information can provide more clues about his learning. Several procedures go into using a search engine, for example, such as inputting information in different fields, setting options, and reviewing output pages. Trouble recalling how to use all of a search engine's features may suggest a long-term memory weakness.

Part of the art of conducting an online search is selecting the best terms to enter into the search engine. For instance, if we want to find material about *sharks* we probably would want to enter some additional terms such as *marine* or *predator* so that we don't pull up sites related to the San Jose Sharks hockey team. (We could also use a "do not include" field to rule out unwanted results.) A kid who struggles with these nuances of online searching may have uneven logic, reasoning, and understanding of concepts.

Once we get the search results, the filtering process begins. If a kid is easily overwhelmed by an avalanche of hits, he may have unreliable processing control, which helps to prioritize details. After clicking on a link to a site that seems promising, we use processing control to review the material quickly, as well as *receptive language* to interpret words, sentences, and longer pieces of language.

Finally, oversurfing, or jumping from one site to another using intriguing links can be very tempting. In fact, Web sites with advertising are designed to lure attention with flashing banners, prominent links, and pop-ups. Kids with weak processing control may have a hard time resisting these forms of technological distraction.

Answering Homework Questions

"Homework consultant" can become a big parent role, especially when it comes to fielding questions about schoolwork. "Who was the third U.S. president?" "What's a prime number?" "What is the capital of Nevada?" When a kid can't come up with an answer on her own, she will often turn to Mom or Dad as de facto encyclopedia. Patterns may emerge in the kinds of questions that are particularly vexing. Earlier in this chapter you met Nabia, a ninth grader who has a lot more trouble with open-ended test questions than with recognition questions. A similar contrast could show up during homework. A kid who asks for help with open-ended, free-recall questions (like the examples provided earlier) more often than with recognition questions may have trouble with *long-term memory access*. On the other hand, a kid who seems to ask for help with recognition questions (such as "Was the first U.S. President Washington, Jefferson, Adams, or Monroe?") just as often as with open-ended questions probably has trouble with *long-term memory storage*, because the information didn't get put into memory banks, so hinting doesn't help.

How-to Questions.   Kids often fire other kinds of questions at parents when doing their homework, and each type can provide clues about their learning. Two such question categories are *how-to* and *what's up? How-to* questions relate to the various procedures and rules that kids need to access when doing their homework. Asking these questions is a tip-off that long-term memory isn't working well, especially if the student can readily use the procedure or rule once prompted (which suggests he understands it). Examples include the following:

- How do I borrow a number?
- How do you spell *summary* when there's more than one summary?
- Do you put the period before or after the quotation mark at the end of the sentence?
- How would I solve for *n* in this problem?

Remember that we're talking about the questions kids ask during homework, not about the answers you may or may not be able to give. The important thing is to listen carefully and let the questions teach you about your child's learning.

Sometimes, however, how-to questions result from something other than memory problems, such as how well the student can reason through a problem. *Applied reasoning* refers to the use of logic to solve problems and tackle challenging situations. A student who asks a lot of deep how-to questions, such as "How would I figure out the amount of water in this canister if this cube is submerged in it?" or "How could I show that climate change is affecting this habitat?" likely has shaky reasoning.

WHAT'S-UP QUESTIONS.   These questions often reveal shaky understanding of the material and of important concepts. They are often accompanied by complaints such as "I don't get it!" or pleas such as "Explain this to me." What's-up questions take many forms, but they all boil down to a less-than-firm grasp of a concept. A concept is a set of critical features of a group of ideas or objects that define that group, determine group membership, and connect it to other groups. Some of the many concepts taught in school are freedom of speech, integers, and symbiosis. Here are some example questions that relate to concepts:

- What's the difference between a cold-blooded animal and a warm-blooded animal?
- What does *extremism* mean?
- Can I just add the tops and bottoms of these two fractions?
- Aren't a phrase and a clause pretty much the same thing?

Table 1.1 lists the clues discussed in this section, followed by their possible neurodevelopmental connections. The Atlas of Neurodevelopmental Terms provided in Appendix Three goes in the opposite direction (lists neurodevelopmental functions followed by their potential clues). The Glossary of Academic Skills located in Appendix Four describes major academic areas (such as math reasoning) along with the primary functions involved in them. You'll notice that in Table 1.1, and in similar tables that follow, up to three possible connections are listed for each clue. The lists are not exhaustive; other potential explanations for a learning phenomenon may exist. The connections listed are the usual suspects, so to speak, or the top contenders.

Locating Clues in Work Samples

The previous section covered what you can learn by watching and listening to your child do homework. This section focuses on the numerous clues that can be gathered by taking a good look at work products, at what is done both at school and at home. When observing and listening to your child you're like an

Table 1.1 *Making Sense of Clues Gathered During Homework Time*

CLUES	POSSIBLE NEURODEVELOP-MENTAL CONNECTIONS	COMMENTS
Pencil grip that isn't tripod	Graphomotor function	See Figure 1.2 for examples
Watching pencil intently	Graphomotor function	May happen because clear signals aren't being sent from the hand to the brain
Jumping into a task too quickly	Production control (attention)	Impulsive work style may rely more on trial and error than on thoughtful planning
Making little, avoidable, or "careless" mistakes	Production control (attention)	When prompted, the student can easily correct the errors
Wandering mind	Processing control (attention)	Mind trips and day-dreaming can happen even without any obvious distractions
Getting lost in the middle of a task	Active working memory	Usually more of a problem when there are a lot of "moving parts" to keep track of
Extremely pulled to nonacademic activities	Processing control (attention); Mental energy (attention)	Fun activities can be very distracting and are far less mentally draining than homework
Excessive mental fatigue	Mental energy (attention)	Can be a particular problem during writing
Not recalling how to use a search engine, including all its features	Long-term memory storage; Long-term memory access	Search engines have procedures for entering criteria and reading the output
Picking ineffective search engine words	Applied reasoning; Conceptual understanding	Trouble with the art of conducting an online search

CLUES	POSSIBLE NEURODEVELOP-MENTAL CONNECTIONS	COMMENTS
Trouble prioritizing search engine results	Processing control (attention); Receptive language	Student may seem overwhelmed by long list of search results; sites have to be quickly reviewed
Oversurfing on the Internet	Processing control (attention)	Many Web sites contain numerous distractions (such as links, banners, and pop-ups)
Hard time with open-ended questions	Long-term memory access	Better with recognition questions, which provide prompts to help with access
Trouble with recognition *and* open-ended questions	Long-term memory storage	Recognition cues (such as multiple choices) prompt access, so the information probably wasn't stored
Asking lots of *How-to* questions	Long-term memory storage; Long-term memory access; Applied reasoning	Procedures and rules may not be stored or readily accessed; could signal difficulty using logic
Asking lots of *what's-up* questions	Conceptual understanding	These questions go beyond memory problems and stem from not "getting it"

anthropologist in the field, on the lookout for revealing behaviors and statements. When reviewing work samples, you're like an archaeologist on a dig, and perhaps the most valuable artifact you can discover is a piece of writing, which you can review for its visual appearance as well as its content.

Handwriting Evidence

Earlier in this chapter I touched on graphomotor function and how some students need to watch the pencil tip very closely because inadequate feedback is sent from the hand back to the brain.

Another way to boost a weak feedback signal is to press really hard on the paper with the pencil to get a stronger sensation of where the tip is during letter formation. So, consistent use of heavy printing is a sign of weak graphomotor function.

Another thing to look for is unusual letter shapes. When graphomotor function is operating reliably, the brain executes a series of patterned movements to recreate a stored image of how a letter should look; but for many kids and adults (myself included!) these movements aren't locked in enough for letters to be shaped correctly every time. The brain is like a computer and the hand is the printer; when graphomotor function is weak, clear signals aren't sent from the brain to the hand to direct the movements needed to shape the letters correctly. As a result, handwriting will contain letters formed in unorthodox ways.

Figure 1.3 contains handwriting samples for students of different ages who experience weak graphomotor function. Each student was asked simply to write a particular letter in a box on a row. Notice how the seven-year-old formed the *a* by combining two different shapes—a circle and a short line—rather than using one motion; the pencil actually lifted off the paper in mid-motion. The seven-year-old also placed letters all over the boxes rather than line them up horizontally. The eight-year-old formed a *w* instead

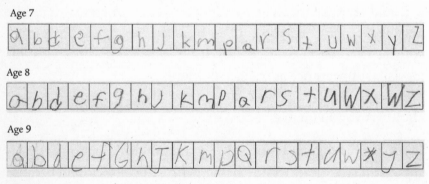

Figure 1.3 *Some Irregular-Looking Letters*

of a *y* in the second box from the right. Both the eight- and nine-year-old mixed upper and lower case (all students were asked to use lower case). Even handwriting that is relatively legible may contain signs of unusual letter formation. For example, a *b* or a *d* may be made with single motions from the top to the bottom and then curving up to complete a loop. Remember that no single clue (such as a different way of forming a letter) is evidence of a weak neurodevelopmental function. You want to gather a lot of information and then look for patterns or recurring themes.

In addition to considering how individual letters look, you can pull the lens back and look at how visually organized the handwriting is on the page. Weak graphomotor function can lead to irregular spacing between letters and words, to the point that determining where one word stops and another starts is very hard. Even on lined paper the sentences may veer off from horizontal, and the margins may stray from vertical. Sometimes the writing can get crowded onto the right side of the page, as words get pushed together rather than moved to the next line. Figure 1.4 shows a sample of this kind of visually disorganized writing.

Spelling Patterns

You can use spelling to tell a lot about a kid's profile by going beyond whether the word is spelled correctly or not and considering the pattern of spelling errors. Many neurodevelopmental functions are needed for good spelling, which is another way of saying that spelling is a complex task. Thus spelling can go awry

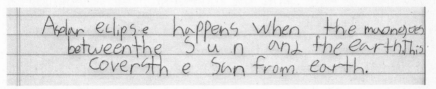

Figure 1.4 *Visually Disorganized Writing*

for several reasons, but let's focus on two major types of spelling mistakes. *Calculate* can be misspelled in a lot of different ways, but one way is *calkyoulayt,* which looks very different from the correct spelling but still *sounds* right. Another misspelling is *calcutate,* which looks pretty close but *sounds* wrong.

A source of frustration for many spellers (for me, anyway) is how many English words are spelled in ways that don't make sense if you focus on how they sound. Put differently, you have to store a lot of mental snapshots in order to spell such words as *Wednesday.* Otherwise, it would be easy to sound out every hard word (and *Wednesday* would be *Wenzday*).

In this book's introduction you met Brady, a second grader who has a hard time sorting out word sounds, such as /f/ in *leaf,* which means he also struggles with connecting sounds with letters (such as *ph* or *gh*). Brady's weakness is with an aspect of language called *phonological processing.* Because his mind doesn't handle word sounds very well, he is susceptible to spelling mistakes like *calcutate* that, when you try to say them out loud, don't sound right. On the other hand, if you see a lot of spelling mistakes like *calkyoulayt,* phonological processing is probably OK because the right word sounds are there. The problem instead is probably that not enough image files for spelling words have been placed in the brain's hard drive. In Table 1.2, the second column contains more examples of this type of long-term memory spelling error while the third column lists phonological errors for the same words.

Writing Rules of the Road

Correct spellings aren't the only things we need to upload into our mental library of visual files for writing. *Writing mechanics* are

Table 1.2 *Examples of Two Kinds of Spelling Errors*

CORRECT SPELLING	SOUNDS CLOSE BUT LOOKS WRONG	LOOKS CLOSE BUT SOUNDS WRONG
cat	kat	cate
badge	baj	badege
laughter	laffter	laughther
swamp	sueomp	somp
answer	anser	anwser
groceries	groshereez	grocercies
catalyst	catulist	catylast

all the rules for putting words on the page that don't necessarily need to be followed when speaking. For example, when writing, we have to capitalize the first word in sentences, separate list items with commas, set off phrases with commas, put quotation marks around spoken statements, use apostrophes to indicate a contraction or possession, and end with punctuation. When speaking, we don't have to follow these rules; we can just let the words flow.

Mechanics rules can be mentally stored as audio files, so to speak—for example, a verbal reminder that sentence-ending punctuation always goes inside the closing quotation mark. But for many learners, these rules take the form of images; we visualize where commas, quotation marks, and apostrophes should go. So, lots of the kinds of written mechanics errors listed in Table 1.3 can indicate weakness with long-term memory or *spatial ordering* (which handles the mind's visual operations) or both.

Writing Vocabulary

Heaviness of print, letter formation, visual organization, spelling, and mechanics are all clues related to the appearance of written work. Now let's delve into what can be learned from the content of writing. One of the first things to consider is word

Table 1.3 *Examples of Writing Mechanics Errors*

INCORRECT MECHANICS	ERROR PATTERN	CORRECT MECHANICS
the water was very cold	Initial capitalization; ending punctuation	The water was very cold.
We need to buy milk eggs and butter.	Commas separating list items	We need to buy milk, eggs, and butter.
Mr. Diaz my math teacher is really nice.	Commas marking a phrase	Mr. Diaz, my math teacher, is really nice.
She said "I have done so much today".	Punctuation with quotation marks	She said, "I have done so much today."
Hes going to carry Camis backpack.	Apostrophes—possessive and contraction	He's going to carry Cami's backpack.

usage, or *semantics* (an aspect of *expressive language*). Writing that contains a lot of misused words, such as using *interval* when *integral* would be the correct choice, can indicate a semantic problem. Another sign of trouble is writing that is very sparse in terms of vocabulary; this kind of writing lacks many vivid, interesting words and may include a lot of nondescript, filler words such as *things* and *stuff.* As I mentioned in one of the "starting pointers" for this chapter, you need to gauge your observations by the age of the student. So, if you have a sense that your child, for a fourth grader, doesn't exercise good word usage in his writing, you have reason to suspect a weakness with semantics.

Comparing Writing and Speaking

Another of this chapter's starting pointers was to take a good look at contrasts in performance, and an excellent example of that is comparing a kid's spoken language and written language. Hei is in the fifth grade and everyone is perplexed by how brief and simple her writing is compared to her amazing ability to communicate when speaking. Take a look at Table 1.4, which

Table 1.4 *Contrast Between Spoken Language and Written Output*

ORAL DESCRIPTION OF FAVORITE BOOK

The Phantom Tollbooth is about Milo, who is always so bored. One day someone sends him a tollbooth that he sets up in his room. He drives through it in his toy car and suddenly he's in this place called the Kingdom of Wisdom. Pretty soon he meets Tock, a watchdog who actually has a big clock in his side. They go to Dictionopolis, where all the letters in the world are grown on trees. Dictionopolis is ruled by King Azaz the Unabridged, and he doesn't get along with his brother, the Mathemagician, who rules the other big city, Digitolopolis. They banished the princesses Rhyme and Reason because they couldn't settle the argument over whether letters or numbers were more important. Without the princesses, the Kingdom is in trouble, so Milo and Tock agree to rescue them from the Castle in the Air, way above the Mountains of Ignorance. And this big talking beetle, Humbug, goes along with them. On the way they go through the Forest of Sight and the Valley of Sound. Everywhere they go they meet different people who need help without Rhyme and Reason. In Digitopolis they meet the Mathemagician and go to the Numbers Mine, where the world's numbers are dug up like jewels. The Mathemagician takes them to the Mountains of Ignorance, which is a scary place with lots of weird demons. But Milo and his friends defeat the demons and get up to the Castle in the Air. But the demons get really mad and chop off the bottom of the stairs to the castle, so they all fly down on Tock—because time flies! The demons chase them but they're saved by the brothers and their armies. After that Milo has to go home and the next day he really wants to go back to the Kingdom, but the tollbooth is gone. At first Milo is sad he won't see his friends there, but then he realizes he can discover a lot at home.

WRITTEN DESCRIPTION OF FAVORITE BOOK

"The Phantom Tollbooth" is by Norton Juster. The main character is Milo, who goes to the Kingdom of Wisdom. He and Tock, a watchdog go to Dictionopolis, the word city, and then Digitopolis, the numbers city. They go save two princesses from demons, and they do it. Then Milo has to go home never to return. But he isn't sad. He can do fun things at home, he thinks.

displays Hei's impressive oral summary of her favorite book, *The Phantom Tollbooth* by Norman Juster, with her sparsely written summary of the same book.

As you can see from her oral description, Hei remembers a great deal about *The Phantom Tollbooth,* she seems to really get the book, and she expresses herself quite well. Her oral output indicates that she has very good expressive language. But if you were to look only at her writing, which is so much shorter and simpler, you would get a vastly different impression of her thinking and language. Clearly something is holding back her language when she has to use a pencil.

When spoken language is more elaborate than written language, the first culprit to consider is graphomotor function. As I described earlier, for kids like Hei the computer is working just fine; it just might not have reliable connections to the printer. Another question to ask is whether Hei has enough mental energy for writing. Again, writing is an extremely demanding task, and she may not have enough fuel in the tank to get her great expressive language onto the page; put differently, she might be taking a lot of shortcuts because she has such low gas mileage. Finally, writing requires a ton of a certain kind of memory called *active working memory*, which is like the brain's RAM in that we hold information there while we're working with it. So many things have to be mentally juggled when we're writing— such as where to put commas, how to spell words, and when to start a new paragraph—that some elements may get dropped if we don't have enough active working memory capacity to hold onto it all.

When talking about *The Phantom Tollbooth,* Hei can just unleash her wonderful, expressive language. But when writing about her favorite book, her graphomotor function, mental energy, or active working memory (or some combination thereof) is likely holding her back. Hei's plight is pretty common

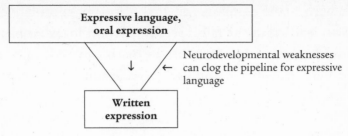

Figure 1.5 *Expressive Language Getting Clogged When Writing*

and can be visualized as her expressive language getting clogged on the way to the page (see Figure 1.5).

A less common but equally confounding pattern is that of the student whose writing is actually longer and more sophisticated than spoken language. Some students' expressive language can generate good output but only at a relatively slow rate. You might even notice this when talking to them in that they may be taking an extra moment to respond, speaking methodically, and pausing frequently. For such students, writing is actually a better way to communicate because writing is a much slower process than speaking. In other words, the pace of writing may better suit some students' slow pace of expressive language.

> Many parents face another obstacle when trying to help their children with school: their own anxieties about learning. This can be especially true for math, which is not a fun subject for a lot of people. If you sense yourself resisting looking into your child's math skills, do your best to set aside your own issues about math.

Math Clues

Let's now turn to math and some of the important clues you can unearth in your child's math work. Math is a complicated subject with many components. It is also very cumulative, that is, what is learned in the fall is very important for what has to be mastered in the spring. Mistakes in math can be grouped into three general categories, and each reveals something important about learning.

HARD-DRIVE ERRORS.   These mistakes relate to problems with memory, and math requires a lot of hard-drive capacity. For instance, students in the elementary grades are expected to memorize dozens of math facts for addition, subtraction, multiplication, and division. Some kids simply haven't uploaded all the facts, so they respond to math fact questions (such as "What's 6 times 7?") inaccurately, if at all. Sometimes, though, a student can generate the right response but needs extra time to do so. If you see this pattern, ask your child how he came up with the answer, because often there was a clever calculation involved (such as "I know 6 times 6 is 36, so if I count up from 36—37, 38, 39, 40, 41, 42—then the answer is 42!"). Now, the student who figures out that 6 times 7 equals 42 this way certainly is a nice strategic thinker, but the fact that he still struggles to recall the correct answer tells us something about his memory.

In addition to recalling facts, students have to store and retrieve numerous *math procedures*, such as how to borrow when subtracting, how to simplify a fraction, and how to balance an algebraic equation. Most math procedures are multistep, and students with memory difficulties have trouble knowing where to start with a problem, or they mess up midstream (such as not shifting the decimal after correctly multiplying the numerals).

NOT-GETTING-IT ERRORS.   Whereas a student who shows a lot of hard-drive errors may actually understand the important ideas behind math, making a lot of not-getting-it errors reveals a shaky conceptual foundation. Finn is a fourth grader who used to always seem to hold his own in math, but the introduction of word problems is throwing him for a loop. He can perform calculations accurately, but he is stymied by word problems, even if they require the same calculations he can carry out in isolation. (See Table 1.5 for some examples.)

Finn's difficulty is that he has a hard time processing the details in word problems, some of which are there only to distract from the important details; he readily falls for these red herrings. Word problems also involve a distinct set of vocabulary terms (such as words that are tip-offs to multiply or divide), and they may include some curve balls in terms of sentence structure (such as listing first the final piece of information you need to solve the problem). So, despite good memory for math procedures, Finn doesn't get word problems very well because of details and complexities of language.

Another kind of not-getting-it math error is having trouble making sense of visual information. Of all the core academic subjects (reading, writing, and math), math is the most challenging

Table 1.5 *Isolated Math Operations vs. Math Word Problems*

MATH OPERATION(S)	MATH WORD PROBLEM
$5 \times 7 = 35$	You need to set up chairs for a group of at least 30 people, and you need 5 rows. If you put 7 chairs in each row, how many chairs do you need?
$3 \times 5 = 15$ $15 + 15 = 30$ $15 + 30 = 45$	Jody earns $15 each time she mows the lawn and $5 for washing a window. How much will she earn washing 3 windows and mowing the lawn twice?
$48 \div 12 = 4$ $4 \times 2/3 = 8/3$ $8/3 = 2\ 2/3$	A cookie recipe calls for 2/3 of a cup of sugar to bake a batch of 12 cookies. You want to bake 48 cookies for a party; how much sugar will you need?

in terms of bombarding kids with abstract visual material. The bombardment starts in the elementary grades with basic shapes and representations of fractions. In the late elementary and middle grades students have to start interpreting charts and graphs. Plus, in the middle grades kids often have to deal with word problems that require diagramming or visualizing how quantities compare (usually via subtraction) or are transformed (with addition, multiplication, division, or some combination). In the upper grades, math students have to handle sophisticated geometric visuals such as angles and polygons, as well as abstract concepts such as tangents and cosines. A pattern of errors in your child's math related to visual information may signal spatial ordering as the culprit.

Finally, when looking closely at math work you might see evidence of one other example of a not-getting-it error: a haphazard approach to problems, that is, an approach that is more trial-and-error than strategic. This pattern often stems from a weakness in the child's attention production control. What you will see is work that jumps right to a calculation or an attempt at an answer. In contrast, a child who uses good planning in math will display stages, such as first drawing a diagram, then setting up equations, performing calculations, and finally checking answers. Figure 1.6 displays an example of planned math work and an example of unplanned math work, both using the same problem. In the planned example, the student started with a diagram (not to scale, but sufficient to visualize the problem's key elements), labeled and performed initial calculations (the area of the field and of the garden), and ultimately arrived at the correct solution; the arrows reveal the order in which the student proceeded. In the unplanned math work, the student just started calculating using the numbers provided in the problem; note that although the calculations were performed correctly, they weren't the right calculations for this problem.

Mr. Vasquez wants to convert some of his backyard into a garden. His yard is 110 feet long and 45 feet wide. If the dimensions of his garden are 12 feet by 10 feet, how much of his yard will be left?

Planned Work   Unplanned Work

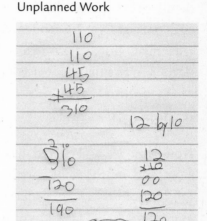

Figure 1.6 *Planned and Unplanned Math Work*

IN-THE-DETAILS ERRORS.   Parents and teachers often pull their hair out when they see these kinds of mistakes because they are so easily corrected. *If he was just more careful he'd get every one of those problems right!* Sound familiar? In-the-details errors usually happen because the student skims over the problem and assumes it's a minus sign instead of a plus sign, for example. He might solve a word problem, setting it up correctly and performing every calculation properly, but still get it wrong because he used 325 instead of 375. He might also veer toward the nonessential or distracting details in word problems rather than zeroing in on the important information. All of these examples are evidence of problematic attention (usually processing control, though inconsistent self-correction can also be a sign of production control weakness). An in-the-details error that can be really obvious in math is visually disorganized work. For instance, not lining up numerals in columns can lead to miscalculations (see Figure 1.7 for an example). The recurring theme with in-the-detail errors is that the student has good memory for math facts and procedures, he understands concepts and can use logical reasoning, but little mistakes are derailing him. Put simply, the devil is in the details.

Dealing with Q and A

Now that we've covered handwriting, spelling, written expression, and math, we'll conclude by discussing the clues to look for in homework in general. The format of many homework assignments is "Q and A," or question and answer. So, when looking through your child's homework for science, social studies, language arts, foreign language, history, and so on, consider the kinds of questions your child has to answer. Questions can be categorized in a couple of ways. First, they can be divided into recognition and open-ended questions. Recognition questions actually display the correct answer in some way, but that answer is mixed in with some wrong answers. Examples include multiple-choice, true-false, and matching questions. The student has to look through all of the possible answers and *recognize* which is the correct one. Open-ended questions don't display the correct answer, meaning that the student doesn't get a cue to help

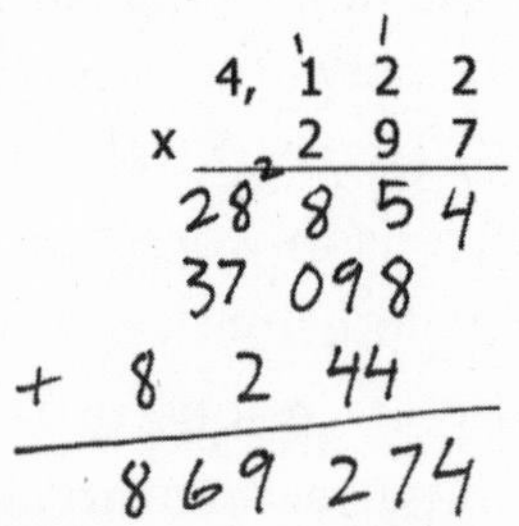

Figure 1.7 *Visually Disorganized Math Work*

access the information. Here are a few examples of open-ended questions, including fill-in-the-blank:

- Which U.S. president advocated for the League of Nations?
- A _____ is a polygon with 6 sides.
- Define *hydrotropism:* _____
- Name the 3 primary colors.

> In addition to homework assignments, include tests and quizzes your child has brought home in your review of work samples.

If you see that your child tends to have more trouble with open-ended questions than with recognition questions, you need to think about long-term memory access as a problem. But if your child does better with recognition questions, then you have evidence that he has stored information in memory; he just has trouble accessing that information without the prompts that recognition questions provide. Nabia, the ninth grader described earlier in this chapter, shows this pattern on her test performance. Trouble with both open-ended and recognition questions can mean problems with long-term memory storage; the information isn't getting uploaded into the brain's hard drive.

Now, some kids actually perform better with open-ended questions than with recognition questions. When this is the case, the difficulty is usually in discriminating between the potential answers and pinpointing the right one; the student might be easily swayed by an intriguing wrong answer, have a hard time deciding between two very similar answers (such as multiple-choice options), or impulsively pick an incorrect response without carefully reviewing all the options. Trouble with recognition questions coupled with better performance on open-ended questions often relates to attention. Even though the information is available in long-term memory (which is why open-ended questions can be answered), the student has trouble processing the details in the recognition questions or has a hard time controlling impulses to jump toward incorrect responses.

Questions can also be sorted according to whether they require memory (such as the factual questions just presented) or *thinking*. Keep an eye out for better performance with memory questions than with thought questions, which push the student to use reasoning and understand concepts. These kinds of questions tap *conceptual understanding* and applied reasoning. The opposite pattern—doing better with thought questions than with memory questions—suggests difficulty with long-term memory and good higher thinking. Here are some examples of thought questions:

- How could some of the problems that America faced during Reconstruction have been avoided?
- What are some things Tony could do to boost sales at his lemonade stand?
- Describe the advantages and disadvantages of biodiesel.
- Compare and contrast socialism and capitalism.
- What might the Mississippi River represent as a symbol (in the *Adventures of Huckleberry Finn*)?
- How do you think Marie felt about missing the last two weeks of school?
- Would a polar bear feel okay in a desert? Why or why not?

Table 1.6 lists the clues that can be revealed in work samples, along with potential neurodevelopmental connections.

Detective Work During Down Time

Looking for clues about your child's learning during homework time and by reviewing work samples makes sense because these

Table 1.6 *Making Sense of Clues Gathered from Work Samples*

CLUES	POSSIBLE NEURODEVELOP-MENTAL CONNECTIONS	COMMENTS
Heavy print	Graphomotor function	May happen because clear signals aren't being sent from the hand to the brain
Irregular-looking letters	Graphomotor function	See Figure 1.3 for examples
Visually disorganized writing	Graphomotor function	Check spacing between letters and words, and alignment of margins; see Figure 1.4 for an example
Spelling that sounds close but looks wrong (such as *laffter* for *laughter*)	Long-term memory storage; Long-term memory access	Phonological processing is probably OK, because word sounds are accurate; see Table 1.2
Spelling that looks close but sounds wrong (such as *laughther* for *laughter*)	Phonological processing (language)	Word sounds aren't accurate and student relies on what the word sort of looks like; see Table 1.2
Errors with writing mechanics, such as where to put commas	Long-term memory storage; Long-term memory access; Spatial ordering	Some rules are verbal and some are committed to memory in a visual format; see Table 1.3
Vocabulary sparse in written work	Semantics (language)	May find numerous uses of nonspecific terms such as *things* and *stuff*
Writing that is shorter and simpler than spoken language	Graphomotor function; Mental energy (attention); Active working memory	Good expressive language may be stifled by weaknesses in other areas
Writing that is longer and clearer than spoken language	Expressive language	Language likely operates well in all aspects except rate; student does better with the slower pace of writing

(Continued)

Table 1.6 *(Continued)*

CLUES	POSSIBLE NEURODEVELOP-MENTAL CONNECTIONS	COMMENTS
Math fact recall that is inaccurate or incomplete	Long-term memory storage; Long-term memory access	Student may give wrong answers or say, "I don't know"
Math fact recall that is accurate but not automatic	Long-term memory access	Student will give correct answers but will take a moment to generate them
Not following math procedures accurately	Long-term memory storage; Long-term memory access; Active working memory	Even if procedures are stored in memory banks, pulling them out and following them can be hard
Confused by math word problems	Processing control (attention); Semantics (language); Syntax (language)	Difficulty determining what operation to use to solve the problem
Confused by math visuals	Spatial ordering	Math visuals include diagrams, graphs, angles, and geometric shapes
Haphazard approach to solving math problems	Production control (attention)	Jumps right in instead of first thinking about the best way to solve the problem
Misreading details in math problems (such as adding in a subtraction problem)	Processing control (attention)	May be distracted by unimportant details in word problems
Few self-corrections	Production control (attention)	Very few or no erasures; when prompted, the student can easily correct the errors
Visually disorganized math work	Graphomotor function; Spatial ordering	See Figure 1.7 for an example
Harder time with open-ended questions	Long-term memory access	Better with recognition questions, which provide prompts to help with access

CLUES	POSSIBLE NEURODEVELOP-MENTAL CONNECTIONS	COMMENTS
Trouble with recognition *and* open-ended questions	Long-term memory storage	Recognition cues (such as multiple choices) prompt access, so the information probably wasn't stored
Particular difficulty with multiple-choice questions	Processing control (attention); Production control (attention)	Can be hard to pick up details that differentiate responses; incorrect options can be distracting
Particular trouble with thinking questions	Conceptual understanding; Applied reasoning	May do better with factual memory questions

are extensions of your child's school experience. But you can also discover a lot when your child is not engaged in academic work, as long as you keep your eyes open. This section describes some of the potential clues you might detect during play and leisure time and during your child's conversations.

Play and Leisure Activities

Your child's choices during play and leisure activities can tell you about his profile. Take Ivey, for example, who is in the eighth grade. When she's not at school she hardly ever goes near books, magazines, newspapers, or Internet sites—pretty much any incarnation of the printed word. Although she might once in a while check out comic books (which have lots of visual material to accompany their words), she much prefers listening to music, creating and designing things (like bead bracelets), drawing, and her new hobby: jigsaw puzzles. The fact that Ivey avoids just about any kind of reading could indicate difficulty with receptive language. The possibility of weak expressive language should also be considered, because none of her preferences for leisure activities involve generating words (such as talking to others or writing).

Ivey disliked show-and-tell in elementary school, probably because she had to talk about her interests, and she prefers classes that don't have a lot of group discussion, such as art. By the way, Ivey's enjoyment of music is really about the music; when asked, she pays little to no attention to the lyrics.

On the other hand, several of Ivey's hobbies require interpreting and creating visual material, so spatial ordering might be a strength for her. Interestingly, her preferences do not provide a huge amount of stimulation, but they do require patient, methodical approaches, so Ivey's attention could very well be another asset. We all naturally gravitate toward activities that play to our strengths and away from those that expose our weaknesses. After all, if given the choice, wouldn't you rather spend your time doing things you are good at than those that are frustrating?

> Remember that one of the starting pointers for this chapter was to focus on gathering clues at the outset. You don't want to base any conclusion about your child's profile on a single piece of information. You need several pieces in order to put together the puzzle.

Conversation

Most kids engage in a lot of conversation, though with adolescents that is likely to be with peers far more than with parents! If your child (like Ivey) doesn't get into much conversation, you should think about language as an area of difficulty for him. But if you listen carefully to what kids say, and how they say it, you might be able to pinpoint specific language breakdowns. For example, think about your child's vocabulary. What is his range of available words? Does he ever use challenging or vivid words (such as describing something as "intriguing" rather than just as "cool")? Does he heavily lean on a few generic terms and phrases, such as "thing," "stuff," and "you know"? Also, think about whether he misuses words, such as saying, "This is one of those *articles*" when he should have said, "This is one of those *instances*." Vocabulary misuse can range across nouns (such as confusing *symmetry* and *cemetery*), pronouns (such as saying "Jake and me will do it together"), and adverbs and adjectives (such as "She spoke real modest").

> When thinking about your child's language, consider the dialect of where you live and the lingo that kids use in social settings. You're looking for a pattern of difficulty that goes beyond the casual misuse of language with peers.

You should also consider how your child puts words together into sentences. For example, does he make a lot of mistakes with grammar, such as with subject-verb agreement (for example, "Every kid in the class want to come to the park")? Also, a kid with language difficulty might steer away from more complicated sentence structures (such as "Before I can even think about playing, I need to get all my homework done") and rely on basic sentence structures ("I have to finish my homework, then I can play"). Another aspect of language is how much thinking is extended through words (thinking through talking, in a sense), which can be called *verbal elaboration*. A kid who puts a lot into descriptions and actively uses dialogue to share ideas and reason through a situation likely has more advanced language than a kid who is close-lipped or who talks in sound bites even if the topic is of interest to him or related to a talent or area of expertise.

This book focuses on the neurodevelopmental phenomena that undermine school performance. Emotional difficulty can also be a factor—a child with depression, for example, may not speak with much elaboration—but other resources should be tapped to learn more about those possibilities.

Although the opportunity may not present itself often, listen closely to how your child talks about something intellectual (you might even broach a topic during mealtime or in the car). How well does your child make connections between ideas, such as between discounts on music downloads and specials at the grocery store, between dumping of pollution and contamination in the water supply, between winter snowfall and summer river and lake levels, and between rises in energy prices and rises in food prices? Seeing a connection means understanding the underlying concept or concepts, such as percentage, the water cycle, and production cost. Also, consider your child's capacity to defend his opinions or thinking. For example, if he tells you that his favorite rock band is the best ever, or that snowboarding is better than downhill skiing, or that he would much rather stick with a traditional school schedule than go to a year-round schedule, how well can he back up those statements? Being able to support thinking with evidence relates to applied reasoning.

During conversation you can also get a read on long-term memory by looking at how well your child recalls information. Is he frequently stymied when trying to recall a fact (such as a movie character's name), and does a prompt of some kind ("Didn't the character's name start with *J*?") trigger his recall? A problem with receptive language can be revealed by not getting what others are saying (such as misinterpreting statements, appearing confused, or asking for a lot of clarification and rephrasing). Finally, the kid who frequently jumps from topic to topic or makes abrupt shifts in conversation may have unreliable attention, because sustaining a stream of dialogue requires maintaining focus.

Reading

Hopefully your child spends some free time reading, either independently or with you. Younger children usually read aloud, which provides a window into some important aspects of learning. *Reading decoding* refers to the reading of printed words, sometimes known as sounding out or calling out words. Decoding is accomplished through a combination of recognizing the appearance of words (a sight word such as *and*, for example) and using phonics, or breaking words apart and attacking them sound by sound (such as sounding out *chimney* as /ch/ /i/ /m/ /n/ /ee/). It is possible to decode a word, to pronounce it properly, without understanding what it means.

When listening to your child decode words, have an ear for what kinds of words tend to pose challenges. Some words are regularly spelled according to predictable sound rules (such as *sandwich, car,* and *galaxy*); but many words are not spelled regularly and violate the rules of phonics, meaning they have to be committed to visual memory so they can be quickly recognized (for example, *Wednesday* and *answer*). Consistent difficulty decoding regularly spelled words raises a red flag that phonological processing may be weak, because using phonics to sound out words is very hard if the individual sounds are confusing. On the other hand, if your child can sound out regularly spelled words but gets tripped up on words for which phonics don't apply as well, you need to consider long-term memory as the culprit.

Finally, you can develop a sense of your child's receptive language by gauging how well he comprehends what he's reading. How strong are connections between ideas in a story or to background knowledge or other stories? How deeply does she grasp the vocabulary? To what extent does he follow and understand different sentence structures? Are themes and symbolism understandable or not? How well does he "get" what he's reading? To answer these kinds of questions you will probably need to have conversations with your child about books and stories. Don't make this process an inquisition; just casually work in some questions as you make your way through the text. Table 1.7 lists the clues that can emerge during free time, as well as possible neurodevelopmental connections.

Table 1.7 *Making Sense of Clues Gathered During Free Time*

CLUES	POSSIBLE NEURODEVELOP-MENTAL CONNECTIONS	COMMENTS
Avoids language-based leisure activities (such as reading and creative writing)	Receptive language; Expressive language	Nonlanguage activities can vary in level of stimulation (such as drawing vs. playing video games)
Narrow range of words used during conversation	Semantics (language)	Listen carefully to the words your child uses when speaking to you or others
Words misused during conversation	Semantics (language)	Think about nouns, pronouns, adverbs, adjectives, and subject-verb agreement
Overreliance on basic sentence structures when talking	Syntax (language)	The most basic sentence structure is subject-verb-object, for example, "I baked a cake"
Tendency to talk only when spoken to, use of very brief responses	Verbal elaboration (language)	Even if the kid has a body of knowledge about the topic, or the topic is of interest
Difficulty making connections between related ideas and points	Conceptual understanding	Such as seeing how the school principal is similar to a state governor
Trouble discussing opinions or controversies	Applied reasoning	Consider the extent to which thinking can be backed up with points of evidence

CLUES	POSSIBLE NEURODEVELOP- MENTAL CONNECTIONS	COMMENTS
Harder time with open-ended questions	Long-term memory access	Better with recognition questions, which provide prompts to help with access
Trouble with both recognition and open-ended questions	Long-term memory storage	Recognition cues (such as multiple choices) prompt access, so the information probably wasn't stored
Difficulty getting what others are saying	Receptive language	Misinterpreting statements, appearing confused, asking for clarification or rephrasing
Problems sticking with a topic during conversation, or shifting inappropriately	Processing control (attention)	Tangential comments might be made that could confuse others in the conversation
Decoding errors with regularly spelled words	Phonological processing (language)	Phonics skills may be hard to apply to words like *tuition, bolster,* and *better*
Decoding errors with irregularly spelled words	Long-term memory storage; Long-term memory access	This possibility is stronger if the student has an easier time with regularly spelled words
Difficulty understanding text	Receptive language	Not connecting to prior knowledge or linking ideas within the text; trouble with themes and symbols
Trouble grasping words encountered in text	Semantics (language)	Use conversations to explore knowledge of words
Confused by different sentence structures encountered in text	Syntax (language)	Use conversations to explore understanding of sentence structures and grammar rules

Deciphering Disorganization

A common problem of struggling learners is disorganization, which can frustrate parents and teachers alike (especially the adults who are organized by nature). Disorganization is often a scapegoat or lightning rod. *If only she were more organized she would do better!* However, disorganization often is just a symptom of deeper neurodevelopmental challenges. You'll be better equipped to pick strategies to improve organization if you have a handle on what's causing the problem in the first place.

Space and Materials

Students need to be organized in both their spaces (room, closet, drawers, desk, backpack, locker, and so on) and their materials (homework, binder, textbooks, and so forth). Unreliable processing control can lead to this kind of disorganization, because an important role of this aspect of attention is to prioritize details. A student who doesn't rank-order things treats every worksheet, math assignment, report draft—every scrap of paper—as having equal importance. The result is a pack-rat mentality and an avalanche of disordered materials. In addition, weak spatial ordering can cause a skewed sense of how materials should be located and structured (such as in piles, pockets, folders, or drawer sections). Weak spatial ordering can also lead to disorganized work on the page (such as elements of a math problem spread out in a confusing way). Of course graphomotor problems can also lead to disorganized written output in terms of legibility.

Time and Thinking

Academic success also requires being organized in time and thinking (such as project planning and allocating time for studying). If a student has inconsistent attention production control, he will have a hard time looking ahead, planning, and practicing quality control. Limited active working memory capacity will make it hard to mentally juggle multiple task components (such as recalling a math fact, regrouping properly, forming numerals, and lining up columns), and if even one component gets neglected, the organization falls apart. Finally, tenuous conceptual understanding will make identifying connections challenging; as a result, two seemingly related ideas, such as free speech and religious liberty, will remain autonomous in thought and output. So, in a history paper, the organization of ideas may be problematic.

Like many of the learning issues described in this book, difficulty with organization may be shared by parents (the apple doesn't fall far from the tree, as the saying goes), but sometimes kids are far less organized than Mom and Dad, which can heighten tension. In either case, it is important to consider what might be underneath the surface of disorganization. The next chapter starts to deal with strategies you can use once you have a handle on a kid's profile.

Bottom Line

If you've just read this chapter in its entirety, your head is probably spinning because of all the information there is to digest; but bear in mind that you can also use this book as a reference and turn to certain sections when needed. Also, as difficult as it is for you to watch your child struggle in school, remember that it takes time to gather the clues you need to understand his profile. So don't rush yourself, and take the time you need to integrate this material into your thinking.

Before moving to the next chapter, on selecting strategies based on your child's strengths and weaknesses, here are some closing thoughts about the process of uncovering a profile.

- Think of yourself as a detective trying to solve a mystery, because clues are everywhere if you have your eyes open. When your child is struggling in school, then you are struggling too. Even so, try to have fun in the detective role.

After all, you're going to come out the other end with a new perspective on your child.

- Bite off just what you are comfortable chewing at one time. For example, take a week and focus on listening to your child's language. Then take another week and look carefully at work samples—a few days on math work, a couple of days on writing, and so on.

- Even though you probably started this journey out of a desire to discover the reasons for your child's learning struggles, don't forget to identify his strengths. As you observe and listen and review work, take note of what your child is doing right just as you identify the breakdown points.

2

Picking Strategies for Home

THE IDEAS PRESENTED IN THE PREVIOUS CHAPTER HAVE GIVEN YOU A
better sense of your child's neurodevelopmental profile. You may
not have all the answers (later chapters of this book are devoted
to how to get the best professional help in this regard), but you
most certainly have some well-informed hypotheses. Equipped
with this better understanding, you can now pick some strategies to help your child find more success with learning. This
chapter describes strategies according to neurodevelopmental
area (such as attention).

Think of the strategies that follow as examples or demos,
because they represent just a sampling. Let them stir your
thinking about other strategies that might be similar but more
aligned with your child's needs and your home environment. I'll
describe several strategy types, such as an organization system,
along with some key features; but you and your child will need
to decide on the particulars.

With learning challenges *there are no magic bullets*. With
knowledge of your child's strengths and weaknesses you are in
a much better position to select strategies; but once a strategy is
selected, it has to be put into place—and that will take work, for
your child and for you. Remember that learning problems are

almost always multifaceted and develop over time. This means that solutions will also need to be multifaceted and given adequate time to bring about improvement. You may see some initial improvements, some uplifting moments of success early on, but be prepared to stick with strategies in order to see real benefit.

Starting Pointers

1. *Think of these strategies as adjustments to your already busy life, not as add-ons.* As the parent of a student with learning challenges, you likely already put in considerable time and effort to support your child. Now that you have a better sense of your child's learning strengths and weaknesses, you can pick strategies that can augment or even replace what you're already doing. Put simply, you and your child likely will need to work differently, not harder.

2. *Be willing to experiment.* Even though you're in a position to pick strategies that are more targeted and based on your child's profile, you won't have a guarantee that a particular strategy will be effective. Although you may be skeptical about a strategy, be adventurous about new possibilities. Also, let your child try something even if you're pretty sure it wouldn't work for *you*.

3. *Look for opportunities to leverage strengths and affinities.* One of the best teaching tricks is to use an asset to leverage a weakness. A common example is to supplement verbal material (such as extended text) with visual material (such as a schematic outline or diagram), which is to leverage spatial ordering to improve language. Affinities, or areas of strong interest, can also be used to make information more engaging and approachable. A sports fan, for instance, may take better to learning math concepts and

procedures in the context of baseball statistics. Also, kids (and adults) are almost always more motivated to read about topics of interest to them, which may mean exploring magazines and Web sites. More ways to utilize assets and affinities exist than can be listed here, so use your creativity to make it happen with your child.

4. *Whenever you can, make it a game.* Renowned early-twentieth-century educator and psychologist John Dewey wrote that being playful and serious at the same time is not only possible but actually ideal for learning. If you look at it from a kid's perspective, after a long day of work at school it is really tough to then take up the same challenging work at home (sometimes for several more hours). So try to turn work into play. Revising a report could turn into a scavenger hunt ("How many misspelled words can you find?"). Memorizing state capitals can be a card game ("Match this state card with the right capital card"). The possibilities are endless, as long as you're willing to try.

5. *Be aware of two kinds of learning strategies.* The first kind is designed to build up a weak function or skill; these building strategies are sometimes called *interventions*. The second kind is a tactic for bypassing a weakness in some way; these strategies are often referred to as *accommodations* or *modifications*. Some strategies can both build and bypass at the same time; others swing between the categories depending on what the goal is. Most students need a combination of strategies—building strategies so they can make improvements, bypassing strategies so they can experience success without being hindered by their weaknesses.

6. *Be transparent about a strategy's rationale.* Share with your child what you've learned about his profile, even if you feel you've just got some working hypotheses (the Atlas of

Neurodevelopmental Terms in Appendix Three includes explanations and metaphors that may be helpful, especially with
younger children). Then explain what you're doing about it.
This will help your child better understand his profile, and it
increases the probability of buy-in because the strategy will not
be "just another thing to do" but rather a tactic that is selected
with a special purpose. If the strategy leverages a strength or
affinity, be sure to point out how.

7. *Be mindful of parent-child dynamics.* You're not just your
child's tutor or academic consultant, you're a person your child
desperately wants to please. Nobody likes to fail, especially in
front of a parent. If your interactions turn negative, back away
and give your kid space. Learning and schoolwork are important, but not as important as your relationship. You might need
to change the pace by alternating which parent is providing the
support. If the situation gets really dicey, consider bringing in
a tutor and staying out of the academic work completely. But
if you're the one providing the support, strive for a partnership that has limits. You can act as copilot, but if you sense that
you're becoming the pilot, you need to step back. In other words,
provide all the support you can short of rescue.

Strategies for Unreliable Attention

If you suspect that your child has inconsistent mental energy,
processing control, or production control, or some combination of these, you can find numerous strategies to help (again,
more than can be described here). Attention plays a major role
in organizing the information that comes in and the thoughts
that we generate. That's why kids with attention problems are
so often described as disorganized. So one way to think about

bolstering processing and production control is to work *outside-inside,* meaning that if you surround the kid with organization (on the outside), then over time habits of thought (inside) will be developed that are more coordinated and systematic.

Working from the Outside to the Inside

MODELING FOR YOUR CHILD.   One way to work outside-inside is to provide plenty of modeling for how to work and learn in an organized way. Households provide many opportunities to show how things can be organized: food pantry, utensil drawer, checkbook, closet, music collection, and so on. Show your child how you're tackling a project in a systematic way, whether for your job or around the house. Some kids need to see how things could be organized.

Think of organization as a continuum, not an either-or notion. Describe it as a 1–10 scale, with 10 being the highest level of organization. Discuss where your child is on that scale (maybe a 3), where you might be (maybe an 8), and agree on where you might meet in the middle (perhaps at 6). Or maybe you and your child are both low on the scale and need to work together to improve. In any event, incremental improvements will seem more achievable than an overhaul.

ORGANIZATION SYSTEMS.   Collaborate with your child to develop and implement an organization system. This process starts with specifying what really needs to be organized and to what extent, which likely means setting priorities and compromising. For instance, getting homework materials more organized probably has to happen, but perhaps let go of the idea that your child's closet needs to be organized (at least for the time being). You can organize with a lot of tricks, such as color-coding materials to categorize them more easily. You can get a lot of mileage out of labeling items and locations, such as around your child's work space. Post photos of how things (such as a backpack, binder, or homework folder) should look when they're organized so that your child can refer to them. An organization system that you create with your child will have a better chance of success than one that is imposed on him. At the outset, you may need to provide reinforcement for using the system (using rewards is discussed shortly) until it gains traction with your child.

WORK SCHEDULES.   It goes without saying that kids with attention problems have a hard time sticking with homework for long stretches, as well as difficulty knowing what to do and when. A schedule can help with this, especially if it is very specific about what happens during each block of time (such as five minutes to look over math problems in order to flag potentially tricky ones or important details, fifteen minutes to solve them, and five minutes to check for accuracy). Writing assignments can be folded into schedules in stages (such as ten minutes for brainstorming, ten minutes to create an outline, thirty minutes to write a rough draft, and so on). A nightly schedule can include slots devoted to long-term projects, and you could have a weekly schedule in which major tasks are covered (such as researching a topic for a paper on Tuesday, brainstorming and outlining on Wednesday, first draft on Thursday, and so on).

Breaks from work really can make a difference, especially for a kid with limited mental energy or processing control. Try different patterns of breaks in terms of length and frequency. For instance, you might find that your child does better working for fifteen-minute stretches separated by five-minute breaks than for thirty-minute stretches separated by ten-minute breaks (or vice versa). Breaks should be explicit components of a nightly work schedule. Think about various kinds of breaks, including physical activity (such as getting outside to run around or throw a ball), mental downtime (such as playing a videogame or listening to music), or instructionally relevant activity (such as spending time on academic work your child actually enjoys). In addition to breaks, transitioning from one task to another can provide a jolt of mental fuel; bear in mind that all the math work, for example, doesn't have to be done in a single stretch. Also, allowing for physical movement during work (such as standing or pacing while memorizing or talking through a task) can help kids with attention weaknesses. Such movement can be on a small scale, such as handling a bean bag or other kind of manipulation toy.

As with organization systems, a schedule will work better if you and your child work together to create it. You may need to experiment with different routines, so be willing to tweak it until you and your child find a workable rhythm. Also, at the outset you may need to provide some reinforcement for implementing a schedule until it becomes a habit of mind.

REWARD SYSTEMS.   Emphasize positive reinforcement, meaning that the kid earns something for desirable work or behavior (rather than taking away things or punishing undesirable work or misbehavior). Effective reward systems have several common ingredients:

1. The system should be set up collaboratively, with input even from younger children. Your child should be involved in deciding what the rewards might be; this collaboration will increase motivation, but parents have veto power over a kid's suggestions ("No, you can't earn a Ferrari").
2. Agree on what behaviors or habits will be reinforced, and choose only things the student can directly control. For

example, good grades don't work well for reward systems because so much of grading is controlled by the teacher.

3. Pick a small number of habits (two or three for younger kids, around five for older students) on which to work, such as:

   ° Bringing home what is needed for homework
   ° Sticking with homework for specified lengths of time, without succumbing to distractions, fatigue, or the need for a break
   ° Developing good plans before starting tasks, such as an outline for a paper or a study plan prior to a big test
   ° Using plans once they're created, such as drafting a paper based on an outline or memorizing material according to the study plan
   ° Checking over work, perhaps earning a point for every good edit in a paper or every error detected in a math assignment
   ° Completing assignments
   ° Handing in assignments

4. Build in lots of opportunities for small victories (such as bringing home necessary homework materials or working steadily for just five- to ten-minute stretches) to help create momentum for success.

5. Install levels of reinforcement, such as 20 points to earn a small reward, 20 more points to earn a bigger reward, and 20 more points to earn a grand prize (you can always cycle back through the levels).

6. Fade the system over time, possibly by stretching how many points are needed for rewards (such as requiring 30 points at each level of reward in the second cycle).

When set up the right way and implemented with consistency, reinforcement systems can yield important and lasting benefits.

Making It a Game

Game-like activities have a way of rallying attention, and you can convert tasks into games in all kinds of ways if you keep your eyes open. For example, checking over work for mistakes could be a scavenger hunt. Finding only the most important details in a textbook reading assignment could be like being a detective searching for clues. Look through a picture book or magazine and play "I Spy." Answering multiple-choice questions could be a game in which your child has to eliminate all of the incorrect answers rather than peg the correct answer. Reviewing material for an upcoming quiz or exam could be like a game show. The possibilities really are endless.

Picking Sports and Extracurricular Activities

Sports vary widely in terms of the demands they place on attention. For example, soccer is a game of near-constant action, whereas baseball has lots of downtime that can be problematic for a kid with limited processing control. But you can look even more specifically at the positions of the players. In baseball, for instance, the pitcher, catcher, and first-base player will be much more consistently involved than an outfielder. This same logic can be applied to clubs and other extracurricular activities; the more continuous the activity is, the less stress there is likely to be placed on attention.

Some strategies can help with multiple functions. Turning tasks into games, for instance, could help with memory or language as well as with attention. So don't be confined by where strategies are listed in this book.

Table 2.1 lists the strategies for unreliable attention discussed in this section, including the specific attention component (mental energy, processing control, or production control) addressed by each.

Strategies for Memory Gaps

Using Different Formats

If your child struggles with memory demands, one of the best fallback strategies is to find the best format for information and then use it as much as possible. For example, some kids have

Table 2.1 *Strategies for Unreliable Attention*

STRATEGIES	ATTENTION COMPONENT	COMMENTS
Model learning and working in organized ways	Processing control; Production control	Opportunities for organizing abound in a home
Collaborate to create an organization system	Processing control; Production control	Set priorities and be willing to compromise; could use tactics such as color coding or labeling spaces
Jointly develop work schedules	Mental energy; Processing control; Production control	Schedules can incorporate breaks, reinforce work expectations, and provide organizational structures
Set up a reward system that emphasizes positive reinforcement	Mental energy; Processing control; Production control	Your child should have input about goals and rewards; set a small number of target behaviors
Turn tasks into games	Mental energy; Processing control; Production control	Can promote focus on detail and planning, and can make work more stimulating (for mental energy)

an easier time memorizing visual material than verbal information, perhaps due to good spatial ordering or because visual formats provide different clues to what is critical and what isn't. For these kids, study guides that look schematic or graphically compelling will be more effective. On the other hand, some kids would be mystified by graphic organizers and the like (maybe their spatial ordering is problematic), so they need to stick with more traditional outlines or lists of information (see Figure 2.1 for a comparison), or even to focus on hearing the information by reading it to themselves or listening to someone else read it or to an audio recording of it. When a modality is particularly effective—and some experimenting may be needed to find it—push material into that format. If all modalities seem to be equally effective (or ineffective), then the overall strategy may need to be balancing formats or alternating between them so that material is registered in multiple ways.

Memorizing visual information is like using your mental camera, and learning verbal material is like using your mental audio recorder. For some, one device works better than the other. For many, it makes a big difference if both are used simultaneously.

Different formats can also be leveraged to boost memory simply through the process of converting information from one format to another. Taking material and significantly altering it, such as creating a graphic organizer (like the one shown at the top in Figure 2.1, for example) from information originating in another format, such as a textbook or bulleted notes, promotes deep engagement. Grappling with ideas and terms solidifies them in memory. So, transforming material when studying can bolster memory in a couple of ways; the conversion process itself

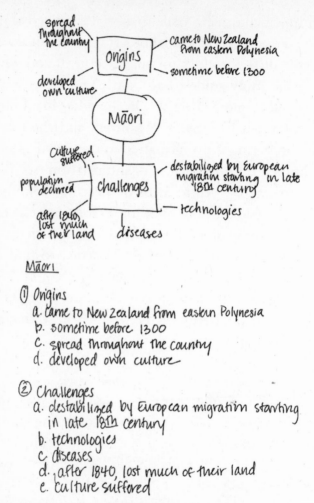

Figure 2.1 *Graphically Organized Notes vs. Bulleted List*

helps register it, and the end product may be a custom-made study guide for review. Numerous conversions are possible, including the following:

- Constructing a graphic organizer from text
- Composing text based on information presented visually
- Placing key information in a table, such as two columns representing contrasting ideas such as socialism and capitalism
- Creating a practice test, complete with answer key

Making Connections

Another mainstay for improving long-term memory is to strengthen connections between topics and pieces of information. Ideally, new material gets integrated into a mental network of previously learned facts and concepts, creating a cross-indexed system of sorts. But kids with memory issues often tend to put information in silos, without thinking about how the different pieces are associated. Such connections can be within the topic or subject (such as xylem and phloem in vascular plants), between topics or subjects (such as xylem of plants and arteries in mammals), or between life experiences and the world (such as xylem and a train the kid rode on a trip last year). Don't assume that your child is making these kinds of associations. Talk about them, make them overt, and provide suggestions if necessary. With modeling and practice, kids can learn to connect information on their own, which will go a long way toward closing gaps in memory.

Study Plans

The essential idea for improving memory is to make memorizing a dynamic process with strategies and tactics that promote engagement with the material. Passive, rote memory is rarely effective for anyone, much less for someone who struggles with memory gaps. Developing plans for how to study makes memorizing more active than simply "going over it." Here are some of the essential questions to answer when creating a study plan:

- What kind of test am I studying for? Will I need to recall a lot of facts (as on a quiz show) or perform a lot of procedures (like a musician or athlete)?
- If it's going to be like a quiz show, what kinds of questions will it include? Fill-in-the-blank? Multiple choice? True-false? Essay? Matching?

- If I'm going to have to perform procedures, where can I come up with a lot of practice problems (such as from math or science)?
- What is the scope of information for which I'm responsible?
- What is the best format for me to use to memorize the information?
- How can I transform the information (such as from verbal to visual format) so that I register it deeply?
- Would it help me to study or practice with someone else? If so, who should that be?
- How can I best test myself to be sure I know what I need to know or can do what I need to do?

Regarding the last question, practice tests can be invaluable tools for studying. In addition to providing feedback about how the studying has gone, practice tests can simulate the actual testing situation (especially if they are timed and conducted without distractions). The dress rehearsal can build confidence and mitigate test anxiety.

Many kids resist taking the initial step of generating a study plan, thinking that it's just extra work and that it would be better to get right to memorizing. When you face such resistance, explain that a study plan is an investment; a down payment is required in terms of time up front, but a significant payoff will come in time saved through efficient studying (not to mention better test performance). Even with such a good rationale, you may need to reward the creation of such plans, as well as their execution (see the previous section for tips on positive reinforcement).

Here's one final tip about studying: there's something to the old saw about memorizing just before falling asleep. Information tends to consolidate better in long-term memory when no immediately subsequent experiences interfere. Put simply, sleep helps information sink in more deeply. So, if your child has some especially important or challenging facts or procedures to learn, use the time just before turning out the lights.

Exercising Memory

You can provide opportunities to practice using active working memory. For instance, ask your child to solve math problems in his head. You should probably start with very simple problems and then gradually add complexity and calculation steps. Problems could build on one another, like this:

- What's 7×8?
- What's 7×8, then plus 4?
- What's 7×8, then plus 4, with the total divided by 2?
- What's 7×8, then plus 4, with the total divided by 2, and then 7 subtracted from it?

Modeling how you would solve problems in your own head will help your child develop strategies for how to make the most of his active working memory. So you could think out loud, explaining, "I know 7×8 is 56, so I picture a 56 in my mind. If I add 4 to that I get 60, so I keep that in my head. Divide that by 2 and I get 30. And $30 - 7$ is 23." If necessary, you can make this kind of practice a game by awarding points for every correct calculation.

Direction-following games provide active working memory practice as well. For example, give your child several things to do in a sequence (such as, "Go to the kitchen and bring back a spoon, but look at what time it is on the stove clock. Come back and hand me the spoon, jump up twice, and tell me what time it was on the stove clock."). As with the mental math practice, you can gradually extend the number of directions. You also can coach your child on strategy use, such as visualizing all of the steps before starting, or thinking about the first letter from each key word in the instructions (such as "K for kitchen, S for spoon, T for time, G for give me the spoon, J2 for jump up twice, and T for time again. K-S-T-G-J2-T."). Table 2.2 contains the various memory strategies described in this section.

Table 2.2 *Strategies for Memory Gaps*

STRATEGIES	MEMORY COMPONENT	COMMENTS
Emphasize verbal formats when studying	Long-term memory storage	Examples include traditional outlines; leverages good receptive language
Emphasize visual formats when studying	Long-term memory storage	Examples include graphic organizers and cluster diagrams; leverages good spatial ordering
Have the student convert study material from one format to another	Long-term memory storage	Could be visual to verbal (and vice versa); student could construct tables or practice tests
Bolster connections between topics and pieces of information	Long-term memory storage; Long-term memory access	Create a cross-indexed system that facilitates retrieval; make connections overt
Develop study plans	Long-term memory storage	Make memorizing more dynamic; anticipate types of test question (such as true-false) as well as content
Take practice tests	Long-term memory access	Simulate actual testing conditions, including content, question types, and time limits
Memorize just before sleeping	Long-term memory storage	Information consolidates better without interference; use pre-bedtime for especially important information

STRATEGIES	MEMORY COMPONENT	COMMENTS
Mental math practice	Active working memory	Gradually make problems more challenging by adding steps; model your thinking
Direction-following games	Active working memory	Gradually add steps to the directions; coach strategy use such as visualizing or using initials

Strategies for Limited Language

Improving Listening Skills

Receptive language is the capacity to understand word sounds, word parts, whole words, sentences, and large chunks such as stories and lectures. It is not the same as reading comprehension. We use receptive language to understand when listening as well as when reading. The act of reading involves a lot of skills related to decoding text, making it a more complex activity than listening. On the other hand, listening is more closely aligned with receptive language in many ways.

If your child has limited receptive language, providing practice with listening skills may be necessary. Because listening doesn't also require decoding printed text (which may also be problematic for your child), it provides more targeted practice with comprehending word meanings, sentence structures, and extended descriptions and arguments. You can provide listening comprehension practice for your child in a lot of ways, the most obvious being to read to him. You may need to pause after every paragraph or so to pose questions about what you just read, make predictions about what will come next, or contemplate how the material connects to other things (personal experience, other books read, movies, and so on). Audio books also provide great listening experiences; you (or somebody) should know enough about the content to converse with your child about it.

Television is a fact of life for most families, and fortunately it does provide a lot of educational programming about a range of topics. Also, high-quality entertainment shows, sports, and news can challenge your child's receptive language (much of this content can also be accessed via DVDs or downloaded from the Internet). Many Web sites convey information via audio, but often with visual supports such as photos and diagrams that can help your child make connections (obviously supervision is necessary when kids are online).

Regardless of the form listening practice takes, here are some pointers for getting the most out of audio media for your child:

- *Push the envelope in terms of difficulty.* You don't want to overwhelm your child with material that is too advanced, but you do want to make it a little challenging.
- *If possible, leverage your child's interests.* If your child is into sports, suggest watching one of the many shows devoted to analysis of games and player profiles.
- *Talk with your child about the material (before, during, and after).* Stretch your child's receptive language by asking questions (you might have to act naive about the subject), modeling the forming of connections ("You know, this reminds me of . . ."), and asking for a summary ("So, what were the main reasons they thought this happened?").
- *Expand expressive language at the same time.* Take advantage of opportunities for your child to improve such things as summarizing, describing, explaining, and supporting an opinion.
- *Be transparent about what you're doing.* You want your child to better understand his mind, and discussing the rationale behind the tactics you're using will promote that understanding.

Coaching the Use of Visual Supports

A lot of reading includes visual material to support the text. Visual support doesn't just take the form of pictures and diagrams. Think about some of the devices you've encountered in this book: italicized terms, section headers, pointers that are offset, bulleted lists, and tables. Although you may not have thought much about these devices, they probably helped you interpret the information more efficiently. Many students, especially those with weak language, need to be coached in how to make use of the visual supports they come across when reading. For example, it may not occur to your child that an italicized term can be looked up in a glossary at the back of a book. You may need to walk through how to use an index or an appendix. After coaching, have your child practice, such as by posing a scavenger hunt challenge ("Find the definition of *plasma* in your science book, as well as all the pages that mention it"). Your child may also need coaching in how best to get information from a Web site, including use of devices such as links, pop-ups, rollovers, tabs, site maps, and internal scroll bars.

Building Expressive Language Through Conversation

Strategies to improve expressive language help kids to more easily and clearly communicate when talking or writing. As with just about everything else, practice makes a difference. But kids with limited expressive language by nature often prefer to say very little. So the first trick is to encourage more elaborate language so that your child stretches and builds the capacity to communicate. You could ask about the day's events, what a television show was about, what was found on a Web site, how a sporting contest unfolded (request a play-by-play), and so on. Make sure you strike a casual tone, because your child may turn off in the face of an interrogation. One way to be low-key is to ask questions as you're doing something else, such as making dinner or folding laundry.

When promoting language development, be mindful of the types of questions you ask, which can vary in terms of how much output is required for a response. Here are three question categories:

- *Yes/no.* Obviously you'll usually get very short answers to such questions as, "Did you eat lunch at the cafeteria today?" and "Did you like that movie?"
- *Multiple choice.* More output is required for these questions, although the response is probably just a repeat of one of the presented options; examples include, "Did you eat lunch in the cafeteria, take your own lunch, or go out with friends?" and "Did you think that movie was terrible, fantastic, or just OK?"
- *Open-ended.* These are the toughest questions to respond to because the question doesn't provide any help other than selecting the topic; examples include, "What did you do for lunch today?" and "What did you think of that movie?"

Each of these questions can serve a different purpose in providing expressive language practice. Yes/no questions can get the ball rolling at the start of a conversation and set the stage for follow-up questions. Multiple-choice questions take a little more work to formulate (because you have to provide potential responses) but can be useful in breaking out of brief responses. Also, you can introduce new vocabulary in these questions (such as "Did you think the movie was dreadful, stupendous, or middling?"). Open-ended questions are what you want to strive for, but they may need to follow some practice or a few yes/no and multiple-choice questions. You can also pose an open-ended question, answer it yourself to model, and then throw it to your child (such as, "What did you think of that movie? I thought it was really slow, especially in the beginning, and the finale just copied that other movie we saw last week.")

Games for Improving Expressive Language

You and your child can play a lot of games that can improve expressive language. One example is the headline game, for which you need a table of contents (from a book, magazine, newspaper, or list of links on a Web site). Pick a title (such as "Price of Corn Spikes" or "New Era of Oversight") and then make predictions about that article or story or chapter. Titles can prompt excellent conversations (such as, "What's a *corn spike*?" "In that title, could *spikes* be a noun or a verb?" "What's another word for *era*?" "What does *oversight* mean?" "Is it possible to have *under*sight?"). You can then go to the text to check your predictions and extend your discussion.

Semantics can be expanded and deepened with games. Check out the educational section of a toy store and you'll find plenty of age-appropriate games that involve vocabulary knowledge and use. Many games are informal and can be played on the fly. You and your child could brainstorm synonyms ("How many words can you think of that mean *hot*?") and antonyms ("How many opposite words can we think of for *fast*?"), perhaps during a drive. You can also change words, such as making them more intense ("How could we change *spicy* to make it sound even stronger?"), or build words from various parts ("How many words do we know that have *graph* in them?").

Parlor games such as Charades are a fun way to provide language practice. Although Charades involves nonverbal communication, you still have to think about the clue, its definition, and how to describe it. Guessing provides practice in quickly generating responses. A cousin to Charades is a game sometimes called Salad Bowl. The first step in Salad Bowl is for all the players to write names on small pieces of paper. The names could come from family members, political figures, fictional characters—anyone whom all the players would have a reasonable chance of knowing. The papers are folded and tossed in a salad bowl. The players group into at least two teams and each team gets the bowl in a round. When a team has the bowl, one player from the team pulls papers out one at a time and describes the name so that the rest of the team can guess it. Each team gets sixty seconds per round. This game provides fun expressive language practice by placing a premium on clear, concise communication (for example, describing George Washington as "the first president of the United States" would probably work a lot better than "the guy on the coin" or "there's a city named after him"). By the way, after the bowl has been emptied and a winner declared, you can play a more advanced version by putting the names back into the bowl and repeating the process, only this time allowing descriptions of only three or fewer words (such as "first American president"). This forces really good word choices (and you'll be surprised how readily teams can guess after having just heard all the names and descriptions in the previous round). The ultimate version of Salad Bowl is to play a third round with only one-word descriptions (have fun!).

By the way, many games can sharpen your child's ear for word sounds (phonological processing). In pig Latin, you take the first sound of a word, shift it to the end, and add *ay*. So *cook* would become *ook-kay*, *blue* would become *loo-bay*, and *talent* would become *alent-tay*. Being good at pig Latin requires clearly hearing vowels and consonants, including those in close proximity to each other (such as /b/ and /l/ in *blue*). Ultimately, whole phrases can be translated (*o-nay idding-kay*, or *no kidding!*).

Digital Outlines for Writing

When generating extended pieces of language, such as for a report or oral presentation, an obvious first step is to generate an outline; but if that outline is in a digital format (such as in a word processing document), it can serve as the backbone of the text. For example, each part of the outline could be expanded to kick-start a portion of the report or presentation. In other words, the brief pieces of text in the outline get converted into extended text. Incidentally, that's how I wrote this book: I started with an outline in a word processing document and then kept adding to it until all the outlined points were elaborated.

Leveraging Affinities

Finally, affinities really come in handy when developing language. Your child will be a lot more motivated to improve receptive language, for instance, when practicing by listening to and reading about topics of interest. Similarly, working on expressive language (both speaking and writing) will be more enjoyable when communicating about an affinity. Affinities can also provide opportunities to improve vocabulary knowledge (think about how many terms can be used to discuss football, such as *wedge* and *interior*). By the way, everyone has affinities, though some are obvious and others require a bit of exploration. If you don't know right now what your child's affinities are, just watch and listen and they will emerge. In Table 2.3 you'll find a listing of the strategies discussed in this section, including the specific aspect of language addressed by each.

Strategies for Weak Graphomotor Function

Problems with graphomotor function can be very frustrating, especially when combined with good expressive language

Table 2.3 *Strategies for Limited Language*

STRATEGIES	LANGUAGE COMPONENT	COMMENTS
Read to, or with, your child	Receptive language; Semantics	Pose questions, make predictions, contemplate connections, and discuss vocabulary
Audio books and other media with audio content (including television, movies, and Web sites)	Receptive language	Leverage affinities by picking topics of interest; have conversations about the material
Coach on how to use visual supports, for example, textbook features such as italicized terms	Receptive language	Create opportunities to practice using visual supports, such as a scavenger hunt for terms
Leverage conversation to practice expressive language	Expressive language; Verbal elaboration	In a casual tone, inquire about the day's events, a television show, Web sites, sports, and so on
Use different question types: yes/no, multiple choice, open-ended	Expressive language; Syntax; Verbal elaboration	Yes/no and multiple-choice questions can get the ball rolling and pave the way to open-ended questions
Play the headline game (make predictions about articles, stories, chapters, books, and so on based on their titles)	Semantics; Syntax; Expressive language	Try to come up with several potential meanings for a headline; talk about vocabulary
Brainstorm synonyms and antonyms	Semantics	Can also explore word parts, such as linking related words and altering words (such as adding prefixes)
Play the Salad Bowl game (teams guess names from brief descriptions)	Semantics; Expressive language	Places a premium on clear, concise communication as well as on good word choices

STRATEGIES	LANGUAGE COMPONENT	COMMENTS
Play pig Latin (take the first sound of a word, shift it to the end, and add *ay*)	Phonological processing	"Un-fay or-fay e-thay ole-hay amily-fay!"
Digital outlines for writing	Expressive language; Verbal elaboration	Can serve as the backbone of the document
Leveraging affinities, such as reading or writing about a topic of interest	Receptive language; Expressive language; Semantics	Everyone has affinities, though sometimes they need to be uncovered

(imagine being asked to do a lot of handwriting in an arm cast). As with most other learning challenges, you can use two general types of strategies for graphomotor issues: building strategies (to improve the handwriting process) and bypassing strategies (to take handwriting out of the equation). One of the building strategies for graphomotor function is improving the comfort of the student's pencil grip. Some experimentation may be necessary: different-sized pencils (including mechanical pencils) can be tried, and a grip can be placed near the tip of the pencil (many grips and mechanical pencils are available at office supply stores). You can also experiment with different kinds of paper (textures, weights, sizes, and styles of line) to find a good fit for your child; for example, some students benefit from graph paper because it provides a clear structure for forming letters and text. Incidentally, graph paper also helps students with weak spatial ordering to organize their math work better (such as by lining up numerals in columns and rows).

Another advantage of mechanical pencils, ironically, is that the lead breaks easily. This forces the student to ease up on the pressure when writing, which improves comfort and endurance.

Bypassing strategies fall into two main camps: keyboarding and tactics that allow the student to communicate through speech. Learning proper technique with the home keys is the best way to become efficient with typing. Many software programs teach use of the home keys and promote speed through games and races (the faster you type, for example, the faster you move a car down a track). Tactics that allow communication through speech come in low-tech and high-tech varieties. On the low-tech end, the student could dictate to you (or someone with typing skills) as you transcribe on the computer; the student should watch the screen as he dictates and then take over the keyboard for editing. On the high-tech end, voice recognition software allows the student to speak into a microphone while the computer does the typing (the software requires a training period to map the user's voice). Such software allows the student to be independent while eliminating the barrier of handwriting.

Strategies for Shaky Concepts and Reasoning

Bolstering Concepts

Another way to describe a weakness in conceptual understanding is to say that connections between ideas, or components of ideas, are not strong. An elementary school student with fragile conceptual understanding, for instance, would not clearly understand the connections between addition and multiplication (both are about changing quantity, multiplication is an extension of addition). A middle school student with shaky concepts may not grasp how all the elements of an adverb (part of speech, whole word, modifies all other aspects of language except nouns, can also modify groups of words and other adverbs, often can be formed from other words by altering spellings) are connected. A high schooler who has trouble with concepts may not get how walruses, camels, and rhesus monkeys are connected as mammals even though they live in three very different habitats; further, they would not see how mammalian features such as sweat glands, warm-bloodedness, and a four-chambered heart are connected.

An important tactic for bolstering conceptual understanding, then, is to target connections among and between ideas. Make them as obvious as possible, display them in different formats, and discuss them in various ways. Solve the same math problem through multiplication and repeated addition; talk about addition and multiplication as teammates or as younger sibling and older sibling; draw up a number line that goes from 0 to 100 (such as a ruler) and jump to different quantities by adding together and multiplying same-sized chunks. Create graphically organized notes (see Figure 2.1 for an example) that display the features of adverbs, examples representing the various kinds of adverbs, and some nonexamples (such as adjectives and verbs). Talk about how a four-chambered heart is needed to pump enough blood through a body, including past sweat glands, in order for a warm-blooded animal to maintain a good body temperature; then go over diagrams that show these features in mammals such as walruses, camels, and rhesus monkeys. Basically, don't assume that connections are there for your child, even if you think they've been covered in school or textbooks, or if they are really obvious to you.

Improving Logic and Reasoning

Applied reasoning can be developed through practice, even through opportunities outside of schoolwork. When you have to reason through a problem, do it out loud so your child can hear your thought process. If you're grocery shopping, for instance, and the store is out of a key ingredient for a dinner recipe, consider aloud your options for dealing with the dilemma (such as finding a substitute ingredient, altering the recipe, changing the menu, or going to another store). When making a repair in the home, such as fixing a cracked bathroom tile or a water stain under a leaky window, talk through the strategies you might use. In addition to modeling your reasoning process, engage your child in the thinking; ask for ideas or for evaluations of your ideas (such as, "Would it be a good idea to rip up all the tiles and start over or would it be better just to cut out the cracked pieces?"). Talk about dilemmas from your own work or life, or that arise in the news or sports (such as how a coach might deal with an injury to a star player) over dinner or in the car. Television shows, movies, books, and magazines contain all manner of dilemmas that call for applied reasoning.

Most toy stores have a section devoted to logic and reasoning games. Some games require solving some sort of spatial puzzle, such as configuring differently shaped geometric figures to form a larger shape. Some simulate mysteries to be solved from a set of clues. Others put the players in the position of making decisions about how to create a functioning business or community. Such games can be enjoyable ways to improve reasoning. Games usually come with age guidelines; if your child is really struggling with reasoning, you might consider games intended for younger kids until improvements are made. When you play these games with your child, don't assume that he will just pick up what you're doing by watching. Be transparent about your strategies by thinking out loud.

Talking About Learning

In this chapter we've touched on examples of a lot of different kinds of strategies, but these are only the tip of the iceberg given all the books, Web sites, and other resources devoted to learning issues. Remember that if you have an understanding of your child's profile you will be in a better position to pick strategies that can make a difference. *Be sure to share that understanding with your child.* Even if you're not exactly sure what's going on—maybe you have working hypotheses or are in the ballpark—be transparent about your thinking. Fold your ideas into your routine (in the car, over dinner, at bedtime) by saying things like the following:

- "Your receptive language seems to be just fine—you understand when you read and listen—but you have a harder time with expressive language, that is, sharing your ideas with words."
- "It sure seems like you have trouble storing stuff in your long-term memory."
- "Your spatial ordering is just amazing; you really get visual material and you can create it, too."
- "We think you might have problems with graphomotor function, which means the signals between your brain and your hand get crossed sometimes."
- "Your brain's fuel tank doesn't have enough gas when you need it."
- "You're great with concepts; you really can see how ideas connect to each other."
- "When you juggle information in your head—with your active working memory—some things get dropped."

You'll notice in this list some of the neurodevelopmental terminology introduced in this book, but pairing such terminology with an explanation or metaphor (such as comparing active working memory to a juggler) is often necessary when speaking to kids. The Atlas of Neurodevelopmental Terms in Appendix Three includes explanations and metaphors that can help with this.

With younger kids you can just stick with the metaphor and introduce the terms later. The preceding list also includes statements that describe strengths; discussing strengths is just as important, if not more so, as discussing weaknesses. By mentioning or describing specific terms, you will be giving praise that is both authentic and concrete. Your child has probably heard plenty of glowing praise of a more global nature (such as "You're awesome" or "I think you're a great kid"), but praise that is attached to an aspect of his neurodevelopmental profile may make him feel a kind of esteem that may be new (or long dormant).

When a kid knows about his strengths and weaknesses, he will have an easier time understanding the rationale behind learning strategies. Introducing and then implementing strategies provides plenty of opportunity to discuss a kid's profile. For example, you could explain, "We need to play this game to improve how well your brain hears little word sounds" or "Your applied reasoning works just fine, but we need to list key math words because you have a harder time with semantics" or "We need to try this kind of outline so that your production control doesn't get in the way of your expressive language." Having insight into the reasons a strategy is being used will increase the odds of buy-in, and you certainly need your child to be on board with efforts to improve his success. Again, make sure you also touch on strengths as you explain how a strategy can help with weaknesses.

Something that can really help your child is to hear about learning struggles that you have experienced, especially if you share similar challenges or strengths. Use the same terminology you use to describe your child to help draw the parallel. Be sure to describe how your struggles have made you feel (such as frustrated or discouraged). Although mentioning how you may have persevered and found success is OK, be mindful of sounding preachy (such as, "If I could do it, then you sure can"). Your child could probably really relate to hearing about how you navigate difficulties in your current work and life. All this will help your child marshal the significant effort that will be required to tackle his learning problems and be more successful.

Bottom Line

Talking to your child about strengths and weaknesses is a strategy in and of itself, and all struggling students can benefit from that kind of dialogue. Here are some other thoughts to close out this chapter on strategies:

- You should feel empowered, because you can do a lot to help your child. Your family has much more work ahead, but you can make a difference and your child can make progress.
- Even though you certainly can help your child, don't feel trapped by a frustrating situation. You may need to divide and conquer, that is, to take on some of your child's challenges yourself and enlist assistance for other challenges. Ask for help when you need it!
- Here are some important pledges you can make on behalf of your child:
  - To understand him or her in a specific and authentic way
  - To put boundaries around weaknesses, to focus on some critical issues rather than letting your child feel defective
  - To emphasize strengths (both academic and nonacademic), because maybe the best thing you can do for your child is to make sure that education doesn't strip away his strengths or pound them out of existence

Conquering Learning Problems at School

"Good teachers use strategies all the time. The benefit of under-standing a student's neurodevelopmental profile is being able to pick particular strategies that have the best chance of getting movement in the right direction. Knowing that profile also pro-vides the basics for conversations with the student, to be able to say, 'This is what I've noticed, what might be causing problems, and what we might do about it.' When students better under-stand their learning and have the vocabulary to describe it, they can start to self-advocate, to take ownership of their learning."

—MIDDLE SCHOOL TEACHER

3

Looking for Clues at School

Teachers obviously are in a position to gather an enormous range of clues about a student's neurodevelopmental profile. They have so much information at their fingertips that knowing where to start can be difficult. Finding clues about struggling learners while instructing a whole class is also a challenge. But going into "detective mode" doesn't need to be an additional task on top of an already huge workload. Rather, it can and should be a mindset used throughout the school day—a lens through which information is continuously filtered.

Such a mindset is becoming more important with the rising prominence of triage service models such as *response to intervention* (RTI), which organizes the amount of support that struggling learners receive into hierarchical tiers. The first tier provides the least support and is usually located within the classroom. The second tier is more individualized support, often taking place in the classroom as well. The third and fourth tiers provide intensive support, usually in a separate setting with more individual attention for the student. The selection of strategies at each tier is an exercise in guesswork without a sense of the student's profile; knowing the student's assets and the neurodevelopmental factors underlying skill breakdowns helps decision making about instruction.

All Kinds of Minds (www.allkindsofminds.org) supports educators in understanding neurodevelopmental profiles in order to build success and foster hope for all students, especially those who are struggling. The kind of thinking described in this book is emphasized in the programs offered by All Kinds of Minds, which also provides access to products and tools for revealing students' profiles and creating learning plans.

This chapter, like Chapter One, organizes possible clues about neurodevelopmental functions into the following categories, which should make the process of discovering and understanding those functions seem more manageable:

- Independent work time, when students are on their own to read, solve math problems, write, research on a computer, complete a science quiz, and so on
- Moments when students are interacting with one another, such as group discussions or cooperative learning projects
- Downtime, such as recess, class transitions, lunch, or any breaks students get from academic work per se
- Student work samples

In addition, challenges with organization are discussed. Most sections include a table listing potential clues as well as possible neurodevelopmental connections. By the way, many of the clues covered in Chapter One crossover to what teachers can detect in the classroom.

Starting Pointers

1. *Don't jump to conclusions!* When a student is struggling in school, some hypotheses often jump to mind, such as learning disability or attention deficit, but keep those thoughts at bay

while you gather information. Many of these seemingly easy explanations are really just labels that wouldn't help the student. An example is dyslexia, which basically just means difficulty reading; many neurodevelopmental explanations for reading trouble exist, and identifying those that are in a kid's profile is far more useful than simply saying he has dyslexia. In addition, what initially seems like the explanation (such as attention deficit) may really be something else beneath the surface (such as weak language, which causes the student to lose focus because he's not understanding all that he's hearing and reading).

2. *Collect plenty of information and then try to interpret it.* You'll do a better job of finding clues if you stay as objective as possible. Aim to gather information from several of the categories described in this chapter. Any conclusions you ultimately reach will be questionable if they are based on a narrow range of data. Once you have lots of clues in front of you, the process of deciphering the clues can start (see Chapter One for an explanation of this process). By the way, be sure that you pull together information about things the student does well, not just about learning problems, because highlighting strengths is just as important as explaining difficulties.

3. *Meld this approach with your existing knowledge about education and your professional experience.* This book is probably presenting both a novel mindset and new concepts about learning issues. Although some of the ideas presented here are incongruent with traditional thinking, which uses labels to explain kids, the vast majority of your knowledge and experience should remain intact. Fold what you learn from this book into your existing mental framework. For example, you have accumulated extensive professional norms about skill development for the grade or grades you teach. You can use these norms to help benchmark the clues you gather, to help decide where a performance falls relative to what's common at a kid's age. Whether the student's

performance is atypical (in either a good or bad way) may be a useful clue about a neurodevelopmental profile.

4. *Getting a handle on a student's profile will help you pick strategies and teaching methods.* Remembering this key point may keep you motivated when faced with puzzling information or conflicting hypotheses about breakdown points. Push your inquiry, knowing that the light at the end of the tunnel is a learning plan with a better chance of success.

If you haven't already, you should take a look at the starting pointers at the beginning of Chapter One, because most of those thoughts for parents apply to educators as well.

Observing During Independent Work

Depending on the grade level or levels you teach, students may spend a significant amount of the school day working by themselves—sometimes for short stretches and sometimes for extended stretches. They could be reading, taking a quiz, writing, completing math problems, researching on the Internet, and so on. Although you have provided structure for these periods in terms of expectations and objectives, the student is largely on his own, providing an important window into his strengths and weaknesses.

Keeping the Energy Up

Some students struggle with the allocation of mental energy. A brain's fuel supply may be minimal, or the fuel lines might get clogged. Think of a time when you have been mentally exhausted, perhaps when you had to stay up late or got up really early, or in the middle of a demanding day. At some point you likely resorted to the tactic of moving your body in an effort to energize your mind. Maybe you stood up and stretched, walked around, played drums with a couple of pencils, or juggled something.

Students with inadequate mental energy regularly feel the way you did during these moments, and they often make use of the same kinds of tricks to rally their energy. So when you see a kid who fidgets a great deal, consider the possibility that he's doing it as a strategy to keep his head in the game. You can ask him about it, because even fairly young kids have the capacity to reflect on their thinking and learning.

The student who moves around in order to maintain mental energy is different from the student who moves because he has a hard time checking his impulses. For one thing, the size of the movements usually differs, with impulsive movements often being larger. Movements to mobilize cognitive fuel tend to occur at a slower pace than impulsive actions (think about the kid who walks across the room to stir up some energy compared to the kid who bolts across the room to get to the front of the line). Also, actions driven by impulsivity tend more often to put a kid in hot water, not just in terms of pushing limits but also with peer relationships. Students with problematic attention production control could be described as having revved-up motors. They fall prey to their impulses all too easily. They rush through tasks to the point that accuracy and quality suffer. They also have unreliable quality control systems, meaning that they often miss mistakes in their work that they can easily correct when prompted, such as in math problems or when writing (spelling or punctuation errors, for instance).

Keep in mind that uncovering a student's profile will help you make instructional decisions. So if a student is in constant motion, it matters whether you think it's due to weak mental energy or problematic production control (or some other cause), because the strategies will differ accordingly (see Chapter Four).

Planning and Organizing

A critical aspect of attention production control is the capacity to think ahead, anticipate outcomes, and build a good plan before starting to work. In Chapter One I described Courtney, a sixth grader whose mother portrays her as a "bull in a china closet." Because she is not a natural planner, she never builds an outline before starting to write, making for some very disorganized writing. Courtney's problem solving method, such as in math or science, would be best described as trial and error. She does not adequately plan how she will solve a problem strategically; instead, she just starts working and if she ends up going down the wrong path, she starts over. Courtney needs to improve the acuity of her foresight.

Listening

Independent work is usually preceded by a set of directions that you provide, sometimes orally and sometimes written (such as on the board or on paper). A student may have a hard time following such directions, for several reasons. If you notice that the student has a harder time following orally presented directions than written directions, attention processing control could be problematic. One aspect of processing control is absorbing detail with sufficient depth for comprehending and remembering. When listening, you get only one pass at the information and then it is gone. Also, the speaker, not the listener, controls the speed at which the information is presented. When reading, however, it is possible to control the speed (that is, to read more slowly), as well as to reread, which allows multiple passes at the information. To a degree, written directions bypass processing control. So if you determine that the student follows written directions better than oral directions, you've essentially conducted an experiment comparing two sets of conditions, with weak processing control emerging as a theory.

A student may not understand the language of the directions at the *syntax* level. Without even realizing it, many teachers utilize sentence structures that are confusing to students with language weaknesses. For example, some sentences present a sequence of actions out of correct order (for example, "Before you write down the names of the mammals, be sure to group them by habitat"). Some sentences are comprehensible only if you link them to a preceding sentence (for example, "Be sure you proofread really carefully. Your grade will be based 25 percent on *that*.") or to a subsequent sentence (for example, "You really need to check for *little things*. We just reviewed how to simplify fractions."). Being puzzled by directions is a red flag for this particular kind of receptive language difficulty.

Independent work is also often preceded by an explanation of important information or ideas. For instance, chemistry lab work often follows a lecture on something like the difference between anions and cations. Explaining what a perimeter is (and how it is calculated) leads into independent math work. Clarifying how a simile is distinct from a metaphor paves the way to the task of identifying similes on a worksheet. Students with limited semantics or shaky conceptual understanding will often have trouble making sense of such explanations without support. Semantic knowledge is important because of all the vocabulary (such as *ion*, *perimeter*, and *metaphor*) that is embedded in explanations.

Conceptual understanding goes deeper than vocabulary, because concepts are about critical features that define a set of ideas or objects (such as polygons or literary symbols). A student could know the definitions of a lot of words but not fully grasp how words are connected conceptually. For instance, Kal is a third grader who seems focused when explanations are provided, and when you ask him to define individual words he does fairly well; but he struggles to apply what is explained. One type of explanation is rarely enough for him; he usually needs to take in ideas in more than one way (such as by pairing words with a diagram) and have connections made explicit (such as how finding the perimeter of a triangle is just like measuring three lines and adding up the totals). Once he has a firmer conceptual structure for holding key information, he is better able to work independently.

The Student's Need for Support

How much support does a student need in order to work independently? The student who continually asks for help from the teacher or a peer usually has a very different profile from the student who hums along without assistance. Some students, like Kal, have trouble understanding the key concepts embedded in academic tasks. Oftentimes the student who asks for a lot of help is grappling with long-term memory problems; critical procedures (such as how to balance a chemical equation) or facts (such as which president succeeded Lincoln) may not be accessible in the memory banks. So, getting a lot of procedural or factual questions wrong could signal weak long-term memory.

The student who asks for a lot of help, because of either a conceptual or memory difficulty, is very different from the student who does not ask for help but still needs prompting to stay on task. Rafa is a junior in high school who has a lot of assets; he's a good writer and voracious reader, and he's very knowledgeable about topics such as technology (he's a whiz with gadgets) and military history. But Rafa's focus all too easily gets pulled off course. High schoolers are beset by numerous potential distractions—peer conversation, text messages, the sights and sounds in a bustling school—but Rafa is even more prone to diversion than other students his age. As a result of his weak attention processing control, he is in chronic need of redirection from his teachers.

Handwriting Evidence

Independent work is also an opportunity to take a look at how a student constructs letters with a pencil and paper. Unorthodox letter formation movements, such as stroking up to form the post of a *t* or *p,* can lead to subtle inefficiencies that can compound into slow and laborious handwriting. Now, it is certainly possible to have perfectly legible handwriting that is generated unconventionally, and the handwriting could even be fairly efficient; but if you have a student who struggles with written output, especially if oral output seems more elaborate or sophisticated, it is worth looking carefully at handwriting motions because graphomotor function could be problematic (refer to Figure 1.3 for examples of irregular-looking letters).

Table 3.1 lists the clues discussed in this section, all related to independent work time. Up to three possible neurodevelopmental connections are included for each clue—not exhaustive lists, just the major contenders. Many of the student behaviors discussed in Chapter One carry over from the home environment to the classroom, so make use of that material as well.

Clues Emerging from Student Interactions

An educator once told me that his three R's for teaching were not reading, 'riting, and 'rithmetic but, rather, relationships, relationships, and relationships. Many factors go into effective teaching and deep learning, but relationships (between students, and between teachers and students) are huge. Schools provide

Table 3.1 *Making Sense of Clues Gathered During Independent Work*

CLUES	POSSIBLE NEURODEVELOPMENTAL CONNECTIONS	COMMENTS
Excessive need for movement (such as fidgeting)	Mental energy (attention)	Moving the body is often a tactic for marshalling mental energy
Revved-up motor	Production control (attention)	Difficulty resisting impulses, rushing through tasks, shaky quality control
Trouble planning before starting to work, overuse of trial and error	Production control (attention)	Often seen when writing, but also when solving math or science problems
Problems following directions	Processing control (attention); Syntax	When oral directions are more difficult to follow than written ones, attention is a likely culprit
Difficulty making sense of explanations	Semantics (language); Conceptual understanding	Usually needs more support than other students, such as having things explained in multiple ways
Excessive need for support (from teachers or peers)	Long-term memory storage; Long-term memory access; Conceptual understanding	Are the student's questions about recalling information or understanding concepts?
Chronic distraction, loss of focus	Processing control (attention)	Consider whether the need for redirection is excessive for the student's age and the setting
Unorthodox, inefficient letter-formation movements	Graphomotor function	Often take the form of stroking in the opposite direction of conventional motion

ample opportunity for students to interact, and those moments provide many clues about neurodevelopmental profiles.

Dealing with Q and A

One of the things to look for during class discussions, small-group work, and conversations with your students is how well a kid understands questions or comments. Problems with receptive language can lead to constant requests for repetition ("What was that?"), clarification or rephrasing ("What do you mean?"), or admission of defeat ("I don't understand"). You also might notice that a student's response (oral or behavioral) just isn't in line with the question or previous comment, suggesting an issue with comprehension. In addition, a student who withdraws from discussion (but who is more open during times that are less demanding of language) may do so because of struggles with understanding all of the language zipping around the room. Some of the students who have a hard time with receptive language or verbal concepts suddenly "get it" when information is presented visually; this can take the form of a diagram, chart, or table; picture, model, or demonstration; and so on. Such a surge in understanding may also signal a strength in spatial ordering.

You may have noticed that you haven't come across such terms as *intelligence* or *IQ* in this book. That's because thinking neurodevelopmentally means considering a student's profile of strengths and weaknesses, not making blanket statements about general levels of "ability."

Let's turn to what students may say during interactions and to how to interpret clues that can emerge from their oral language. For instance, Seung is a tenth grader who displays terrific expressive language in terms of word choice, sentence structure, and overall articulation. The problem is that Seung regularly directs his language toward topics that are tangential to the issue at hand. If the class is talking about the industrial revolution, for example, he might comment that air pollution is a concern for athletes training in some parts of the world. In his mind, Seung has made the connection from industrial to industry to factories to pollution to air pollution to breathing to athletes currently in training. To be sure, we want students to make connections between ideas—doing so forms the basis for concepts and innovative thinking—but if the connections often stray so far as to be tangents, something may be awry with attention processing control. On the other hand, the student who struggles to make connections at all (such as seeing how balancing a chemical equation is similar to balancing an algebra equation, or seeing how perimeter and circumference are essentially the same idea applied to different geometric shapes) likely has shaky conceptual understanding.

Getting Ideas Out

Determining when a student understands what's going on is usually fairly easy, even if he's having a hard time sharing his thinking with words. The light bulb is on, so to speak, but words may not flow. Expressive language weaknesses can take several forms, but all of these can hamper how well a student can convey ideas. Some students experience word retrieval problems, meaning they have a hard time pulling up specific words for situations. We've all experienced the tip-of-the-tongue phenomenon, when you know you know the word you need but can't recall it on the spot; so imagine life for someone who goes through that on a regular basis. To get around a word retrieval problem, one might substitute a generic term (such as *thing, stuff, thing-a-ma-jig,* or *whatchamacallit*), call up the wrong word (such as saying *promotion* instead of *probation*), or try to describe the word instead ("You know what I mean: the scientist guy who is a kind of biologist but only studies plants," instead of *botanist*).

Expressive language difficulty can also strike at the sentence level. A student experiencing issues with syntax will probably stick to the basics in terms of sentence structure—relatively few words per sentence, conventional word order (subject-verb-object), few subordinate clauses. Here's how a seventh grader with solid syntax might talk about the use of animals in drug research: "Animal research may have made sense before we had such powerful computers. Now we can conduct a lot of experiments with software to see how drugs might affect cells and tissues. That way we can be more sure a drug is safe before trying it out with people." Clearly this seventh grader has some good ideas, and they are conveyed articulately. Here's another seventh grader who also has good ideas about this topic but struggles with syntax: "We shouldn't research on animals. What if a drug works on an animal but not on a person? We might hurt animals with drugs and then hurt humans too. It's just not worth it."

Another aspect of expressive language to consider is the degree of elaboration. Some students understand concepts and can recall information and formulate sentences, but their natural inclination is to use as few words as possible. Though brevity often is a virtue, being able to describe one's thinking thoroughly, or even extend it through speech, is usually a commodity in school. Both of the following statements contain some essential ingredients for responding to a question about U.S. electoral politics, but they vary greatly in terms of elaboration:

1. The electoral college is a bad idea because someone can become president who got fewer votes than the other person.
2. The electoral college may have made sense when the Constitution was written, but it doesn't now. It's possible

to become president by winning only a small number of states—the ones with the most electoral votes. We've even elected presidents who lost the popular vote.

Both of the students who made these statements would probably fare well on short-answer or multiple-choice tests about this topic, but the student who made statement two would add more to a class discussion and would be more successful on an essay test about electoral politics.

Memory Capacity

Chapter One covered the difference between long-term memory storage and access, and how each is tapped differently depending on the structure of questions. If a student frequently stumbles over open-ended questions (such as "What is the capital of Nevada?") but does much better with recognition questions (such as "What is the capital of Nevada—Las Vegas, Carson City, Helena, or Reno?") then you have good reason to think that long-term memory access is unreliable, even if long-term memory storage is solid; the information is available, but it isn't easily retrieved without prompts or recognition questions such as multiple choice. Students who have just as much difficulty with recognition questions likely did not store the information in the first place. In addition to applying to general information, this pattern can also play out with math facts. For example, the student who has a hard time recalling what 9×8 equals unless given multiple-choice options (such as 70, 72, 76, and 81) probably has stored the correct number (72) but struggles with access.

Speaking of math, a good gauge of a student's active working memory bandwidth is the ease with which mental math calculations are performed. A kid who can compute, without paper and pencil or calculator, that if you "multiply 8 by 2, then subtract 6, double that, and divide by 5, and you get 4," has pretty good active working memory. However, the student who gets mixed up with mental math or has to write every calculation on paper probably has limited working memory capacity.

Comparing Reading and Listening

You might notice during student interactions a discrepancy between listening comprehension and reading comprehension. The student who has an easier time understanding when listening than when reading likely has suspect decoding skills and phonics. Understanding when listening suggests good receptive language, but trouble decoding printed words may be due to problematic phonological processing or long-term memory of the sound-symbol links in our phonics system.

The student who has an easier time comprehending when reading than when listening, however, probably has solid decoding and phonics skills (suggesting intact phonological processing as well as long-term memory). When listening you usually have little control over the rate at which information comes, and you don't have the option of pausing and going back over material as you would when rereading. Consequently, listening can put more stress on attention processing control because the details need to be absorbed deeply on the first pass. Also, any weaknesses in receptive language will be exposed more when listening than when reading. If you are having a hard time understanding language, you're going to benefit from repeated exposures, and these are easier to get through re-reading than when listening to someone talk.

Both listening and reading can be compromised by limited active working memory. To comprehend incoming information, the reader or listener has to connect new ideas to each other as well as to prior knowledge. Active working memory is where these connections take place. A student with weak active working memory may forget details from the beginning of a passage by the end; this might manifest in missing what seem to be obvious connections between ideas (such as details about a story's character, a plot event, a science concept, or a math procedure).

Table 3.2 presents clues that can emerge during various student interactions, along with what they might reveal about neurodevelopmental functions.

Table 3.2 *Making Sense of Clues Gathered During Interactions*

CLUES	POSSIBLE NEURODEVELOP- MENTAL CONNECTIONS	COMMENTS
Confused by questions and comments	Receptive language; Conceptual understanding	Asking for clarification or rephrasing, misinterpreting questions or statements
Need for visual augmentation of verbal material	Receptive language	Can be a sign of good spatial ordering
Problems sticking with a discussion topic, shifting inappropriately	Processing control (attention)	Often takes the form of tangential comments
Difficulty making connections between related ideas and points	Conceptual understanding	Such as seeing how changes in weather patterns can affect an economy
Trouble with efficiently retrieving the right words	Expressive language	May take the form of hesitation ("tip of the tongue") or inaccurate word choice
Overreliance on basic sentence structures when talking	Syntax (language)	May rarely use dependent clauses or may alter conventional word order
Trouble formulating elaborate responses or comments	Verbal elaboration (language)	Assuming the student has a body of knowledge about the topic

CLUES	POSSIBLE NEURODEVELOP-MENTAL CONNECTIONS	COMMENTS
Harder time with open-ended questions	Long-term memory access	Better with recognition questions, which provide prompts to help with access
Trouble with recognition *and* open-ended questions	Long-term memory storage	Recognition cues (such as multiple choices) prompt access, so the information probably wasn't stored
Limited capacity to perform mental math calculations	Active working memory	Student may strongly prefer using pencil and paper to mental calculations ("I have to write this down!")
Easier time comprehending when listening than when reading	Phonological processing (language); Long-term memory storage; Long-term memory access	Weak phonics could be hindering the student's capacity to decode and in turn interpret text
Easier time comprehending when reading than when listening	Processing control (attention); Receptive language	The reader can control the pace and reread when needed; the listener has little control over the pace
Forgetting pieces of information while reading or listening	Active working memory	May manifest as limited connections between ideas within a passage or between new ideas and prior knowledge

Detective Work During Downtime

The previous section focused on what could be learned by observing how students interact with each other and with teachers during academic tasks. A great deal can also be gleaned about a student's profile, particularly with regard to language, by listening in during downtime or when the student is not directly engaged in schoolwork. Examples include recess, lunch, breaks between classes, transitions within lessons, and before and after the school day. But don't cross the line into being intrusive.

In other words, keep your ears open for potential clues while being mindful of students' privacy.

A big potential clue is the extent of social interaction that a student seeks. Of course a student might be withdrawn for a number of reasons, including a shy disposition, limited social skills, a preference for solitude, or even emotional difficulty. Setting aside those possibilities, avoiding social interaction can be a sign of limited language capacity. The nature of kids' conversations—with their rapid exchanges, radically shifting topics, and idiosyncratic vocabulary—reveals how linguistically demanding socializing can be. So a student who struggles with language may very well steer clear of situations in which that weakness would be exposed.

Another way that a student's preferences may reveal a language weakness is activity choice. Numerous activities deemphasize language, such as drawing, sports, and certain games (such as checkers, chess, cards, and so on). Many of these activities not only are relatively less threatening in terms of language demands, but also are opportunities to showcase strengths in other neurodevelopmental functions, such as spatial ordering and applied reasoning. So a different set of possibilities exists for a student who avoids social downtime in order to read, which suggests solid receptive language, and the student who gravitates to sketching or playing Tetris.

> I still remember learning the meaning of the term *diss* from a fifth grader several years ago. I had no idea what it meant, but now it is a commonly known term.

Students who do choose to engage with peers may illuminate particular language weaknesses during their interactions. For example, you might notice a student struggle with some of the lingo of social language. English vocabulary is continuously morphing (a verb that wasn't commonly used until about twenty years ago), and this is especially true for social language, to which terms are regularly added that then fade from usage. Think of some of the synonyms for *excellent* that have come and gone (such as *groovy, psych, phat*, and *snap*), and countless more will come and go. If you hear a student steer clear of the terminology of the day, or misuse it, then you have a piece of evidence that language is a weak area.

Finally, a big tip-off that language may be problematic is difficulty with behavior and conflict resolution. Language allows us to communicate our needs, to voice concerns, and to suggest ways of getting through dilemmas. Students with language problems have been shown often to have coexisting social-behavioral difficulty, in large part because they have to resort to inappropriate means for navigating disagreements. For instance, a student grabs something instead of asking for it or suggesting taking turns. Of more concern is that a student may use physical aggression because he doesn't have the verbal tools to resolve a conflict. What's more, language also serves the role of mediating our thinking. Talking through a tough situation, or thinking through it verbally (having an internal dialogue), inherently slows things down, which helps to avoid ill-advised impulses and to promote good decisions. In essence, language strengthens the brakes of attention production control. So, when you see a student who has chronic difficulty with conflicts and behavior, consider the possibility that weak language may be the culprit.

Locating Clues in Work Samples

In Chapter One I likened reviewing student work to an archaeological dig, and teachers certainly have a treasure trove at their disposal. As you collect clues about a student's neurodevelopmental profile, remember that you are looking for a pattern of evidence.

You want to avoid basing a conclusion on a single, isolated bit of information. By looking across a span of work and viewing it alongside what you are seeing and hearing in student behavior, you'll have enough clues for themes to emerge.

Writing

Writing is a huge area to review, including not only writing assignments per se (such as book reports, stories, essays, and term papers) but also worksheets, tests and quizzes, workbook entries, notebooks, and so on. Basically, any time a student puts pencil to paper, potential clues are left behind about strengths and weaknesses. Let's first cover the appearance of written work (such as spelling and mechanics) and then shift to its content.

SPELLING AND MECHANICS.   An important distinction to note is the spelling of isolated words (such as on a spelling test) and the spelling of words in context. Some students are significantly more accurate when spelling in isolation than when composing sentences or paragraphs. This discrepancy raises the possibility of restricted capacity of active working memory. Writing is a complex task comprising numerous subskills (such as vocabulary use, letter formation, punctuation, idea generation, and so on). Active working memory mentally juggles all of these components, keeping these balls in the air, so to speak. Spelling in isolation is a bit like tossing up one ball at a time, but spelling in context puts several balls in the air at once. Limited working memory means that some balls will get dropped, and spelling accuracy is often what hits the ground.

As mentioned earlier, you can tease apart long-term memory storage and access by comparing how students perform on free recall questions and recognition questions. This comparison can come into play with spelling as well, because long-term memory is critical for using common letter patterns (such as *-tion* and *-ght*) and following common rules (such as *i* before *e* except after *c*). Asking a student to spell *righteous* taps both long-term memory storage and retrieval; but asking a student which of the following is the correct spelling of *righteous* focuses on long-term memory storage: *richeyous, righteous, rightous,* or *rigeous.* A student who consistently does better with recognition spelling than with recall spelling is probably showing good long-term memory storage for letter patterns and rules but weak access to this information without the prompts that recognition cues provide. On the other hand, spelling difficulty that extends into multiple-choice formats suggests that both storage and access are problematic. By the way, spell-checkers in word processors ask students to recognize whether a spelling is correct.

A perplexing situation for many teachers is inconsistent accuracy in spelling and mechanics. Inconsistency, that is, sometimes showing skills that are right on target while other times falling apart, is often a red flag for attention problems, particularly production control. In these situations, the student's internal self-monitor seems to flicker on and off, meaning that easily correctable mistakes slip into the work. Another possibility is limited capacity of active working memory. Take a look at an excerpt in Figure 3.1 from Monika, a seventh grader mentioned in Chapter One. On a test, Monika was asked to describe how cacti have adapted for survival in desert habitats. Due to limited active working memory, she has trouble simultaneously spelling, applying mechanics rules, thinking about a cactus's features, and doing all of the other things that writing requires. As a result, her accuracy in spelling and punctuation is very uneven. In the first sentence she uses commas correctly to set off a phrase, but in the second sentence she doesn't. She also misspells a word (*cacti*) she had just spelled correctly, and she even misspells the same word a couple of different ways (*cactie* and *cactei*).

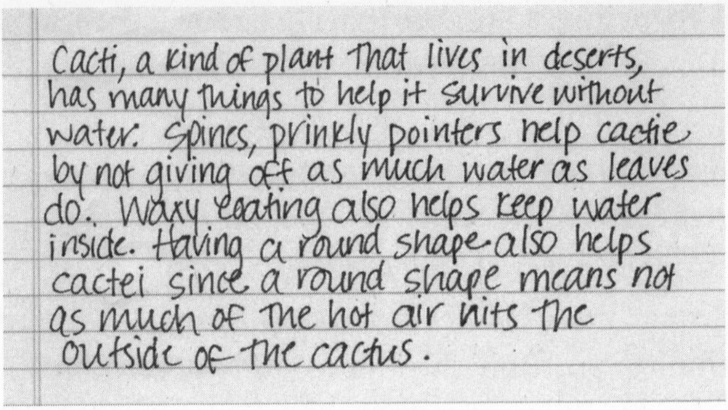

> Cacti, a kind of plant That lives in deserts, has many things to help it survive without water. Spines, prinkly pointers help cactie by not giving off as much water as leaves do. Waxy eeating also helps keep water inside. Having a round shape also helps cactei since a round shape means not as much of the hot air hits the outside of the cactus.

Figure 3.1 *Inconsistent Spelling and Mechanics*

Put differently, Monika's working memory can handle some of the tasks of writing composition, but spelling and mechanics aren't among them.

Some students are much more adept at correcting mechanical and spelling errors while editing than at correctly applying mechanics rules and spelling while composing. This discrepancy might appear when editing their own work, especially if time has passed since the drafting stage, or when editing someone else's writing. This scenario often stems from weak long-term memory access (for spelling and mechanics) coupled with good memory storage. Identifying errors in writing is akin to a recognition task, whereas composing is like a free recall task; as mentioned previously, free recall taps both storage and access while recognition factors out access and focuses on the information that has been stored. This pattern may be particularly obvious in any sort of multiple-choice exercise that requires students to select which sentence contains the correct punctuation, as in this sample item:

a. Jamie told his friend, "Its going to take a long time to get there."

b. Jamie told his friend "It's going to take a long time to get there."

c. Jamie told his friend, "It's going to take a long time to get there."

d. Jamie told his friend, "It's going to take a long time to get there".

The student who can consistently select correct multiple-choice answers (in this item, c) but still struggles with spelling and punctuation when writing is displaying evidence of good memory storage but weak access. This example also illustrates how important attention processing control is for multiple-choice questions, which require picking up on small details (such as the presence or absence of a comma).

CONTENT.   You may recall Ivey, an eighth grader described in Chapter One who prefers leisure activities that require hardly any language, such as drawing and jigsaw puzzles. Figure 3.2 contains an excerpt from a paper she wrote that summarizes her civics class's recent field trip to her state's capitol building. You'll notice that in addition to a fairly narrow range of vocabulary, she sticks with very basic sentence structures. Ivey's writing is indicative of limited expressive language.

As it turns out, the quality of Ivey's written output is similar to that of her speech, which makes an expressive language problem

On Tuesday our civics class went to the state's capitol. It was a huge building with a dome on top. First we went to a big room where laws are voted on. Then we saw someone give a speech. Next we saw someone stand up and not agree with that speech. And then came the vote. Finally, we saw the people get ready to leave the big room where they voted.

Figure 3.2 *Weak Syntax in Writing*

an even more likely possibility. But some students show much more elaborate and sophisticated oral output than written output (recall Hei, from Chapter One, whose oral and written summaries of *The Phantom Tollbooth* are displayed in Table 1.4). When a student can effectively communicate orally, expressive language is on target. When writing quality slips relative to speech, then problems with functions such as graphomotor function, mental energy, and active working memory need to be considered; weaknesses in such functions can clog the pipeline, preventing good expressive language from making it to the page.

Students are often asked to take a stand on an issue, such as how to protect endangered species. Simply stating one's opinion, though, is seldom enough. Assignments and questions usually require backing up an opinion, that is, posing and then defending an argument with evidence. Doing so requires a sophisticated level of thinking, and students who struggle with this may have problems with applied reasoning. Rather than citing supportive evidence, a student with weak reasoning may simply rephrase the opinion or repeat that the issue is important. Figure 3.3 contains an excerpt of writing from Macaria, a high school senior who was asked to describe why a free press is important in a democracy. Although weak expressive language can also lead to problems when arguing an issue with sufficient

---

Free press is a critical aspect of any democracy. The press, or media, need to be able to freely express opinions. Without openness, a closed mentality can arise that is not good for democracy. The founding fathers may not have known about all the types of media, like television or the web, but they knew that the press had to be free. Freedom in the press leads to freedom in the nation.

Figure 3.3 *Tenuous Applied Reasoning in a Writing Sample*

depth, Macaria's writing actually shows solid language in terms of vocabulary and syntax, but her writing is thin in terms of reasoning.

Even with expressive language and reasoning in place, ideas need to be organized for optimal writing. In Chapter One you were introduced to Courtney, a sixth grader for whom planning is a major issue. Specifically, Courtney rarely, if ever, starts her writing process by constructing an outline. Rather, she just starts right into a draft without much forethought. So even though she has unique insights to offer, her terrific ideas typically get lost in a deluge of disorganization on the page. Courtney's attention production control significantly hampers her language, conceptual understanding, and applied reasoning.

Finally, students need to take ideas and expand on them in their writing. Put differently, they need to use language (specifically, verbal elaboration) as a process for thinking. Writing samples that are not well elaborated (that don't seem to go anywhere) are evidence of weak verbal elaboration. This evidence is more compelling if the writing is similar in quality to the student's oral language, suggesting that the other factors (such as active working memory or graphomotor function) are not limiting written output.

Math

Long-term memory is a critical ingredient for math, especially for recalling various procedures. If memory storage is intact but access is weak, then the student will show a pattern of better recognition than recall. This pattern could play out in math work in terms of better performance when some sort of prompt is provided for the necessary procedures. Such prompts could take the form of multiple-choice options, a bank of potential procedures or formulae, or open-note or open-book tests or quizzes.

As important as long-term memory is for math, it can take you only so far. To truly succeed in math you have to understand what you're doing, which is why conceptual understanding is important. All but the most talented mathematicians have experienced, at some point in their schooling, following a procedure or algorithm without understanding how or why it worked. For example, many math students know the Pythagorean theorem, $a^2 + b^2 = c^2$, and that it is used to calculate one length of a right triangle given the other two lengths. A key component of this procedure is that c represents the length of the hypotenuse, or the length that is opposite the right (90-degree) angle. All of these details can be committed to memory and used to calculate answers to problems. But how many students understand the deeper ideas behind this theorem? Where did this theorem originate? Why does a^2 plus b^2 equal c^2? (In case you're wondering, it has to do with the collective areas of three squares pushed together so that their sides form a triangle with a right angle.)

Granted, this may be an extreme example, because a lot of people have no trouble using the Pythagorean theorem without knowing its origins. It does illustrate the difference between memory and understanding in math. Some students, even those earning solid grades, have perfectly good long-term memory but tenuous understanding of the foundational ideas in math, such as that subtraction is the opposite of addition, why dividing by a fraction is the same as multiplying by the inverse of that fraction, where pi comes from, the distinction between natural numbers and integers, the connection between slope expressed algebraically ($y = mx + b$) and slope displayed on a graph, and so on.

Students with better memory than understanding in math will show particular signs in their work. One is much better success applying a procedure or algorithm in a familiar situation than in a novel scenario. When faced with the familiar, working by rote can lead to success, but new types of problems usually require a deeper level of understanding or the capacity to use reasoning and logic to discover a solution. Also, shaky conceptual understanding can surface when problems combine foundational ideas, in contrast to practice problems that isolate particular concepts. So a student with decent memory may be able to convert a mixed fraction into an improper fraction, and may know that inverting a fraction is a key step when dividing by a fraction, but a word problem involving both of these ideas could be a hurdle if that student doesn't get the concepts.

Another way that tenuous conceptual understanding reveals itself in math is through the quality of diagrams the student uses to solve problems. Most students are coached to construct a diagram to help sort out the elements of a problem and identify necessary procedures, but a student who doesn't get concepts in the first place is going to be at a loss as to how to visualize the problem and display it graphically. To that student, the "draw a picture" tactic will probably involve creating images of the problem elements that do not convey values or relationships between values. Figure 3.4 contains an example of a word problem and two student diagrams, one pictorial and one schematic. The schematic diagram, unlike the pictorial, shows how the essential problem details connect, and paves the way to the solution (adding 8, 6, and 7 blocks to calculate distance traveled on the bike).

Table 3.3 includes clues that can be identified in student work samples, including potential associated neurodevelopmental functions.

Deciphering Disorganization

Disorganization is often an outgrowth of a neurodevelopmental profile. Challenges with functions such as attention processing control and spatial ordering can lead to disorganized space and materials (such as desk, locker, binder, backpack, and so on)

After school Deanna rode her bike 8 blocks from her home to the park. Then she rode to the pond, which is 9 blocks from the park. The pond is 6 blocks from home. After riding home from the pond, how many blocks did she ride all together?

PICTORIAL DIAGRAM   SCHEMATIC DIAGRAM

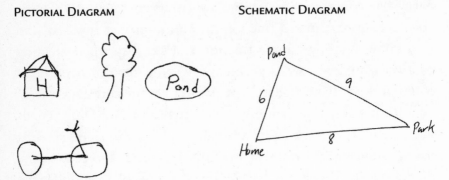

Figure 3.4 *Pictorial vs. Schematic Diagrams for Math Problem Solving*

Table 3.3 *Making Sense of Clues Gathered from Work Samples*

CLUES	POSSIBLE NEURODEVELOP-MENTAL CONNECTIONS	COMMENTS
Spelling accuracy better with isolated words than with words in context	Active working memory	Composing sentences and paragraphs requires mentally juggling numerous tasks
Better recognition spelling than recall spelling	Long-term memory access	Recognition format (such as multiple choice) provides prompts to help with long-term memory access
Inconsistent spelling and written mechanics	Production control (attention); Active working memory	The culprit may be unreliable self-monitoring or quality control
Easier time editing than using mechanics independently	Long-term memory access	Editing involves recognizing elements of mechanics, as opposed to free recall
Overreliance on basic sentence structures when writing	Syntax (language)	May rarely use dependent clauses or may alter conventional word order to enhance writing

CLUES	POSSIBLE NEURODEVELOP-MENTAL CONNECTIONS	COMMENTS
Written output that is less sophisticated than oral output	Graphomotor function; Mental energy (attention); Active working memory	Good expressive language may be stifled by weaknesses in other areas, such as graphomotor function
Trouble posing and defending arguments in writing	Applied reasoning; Expressive language	Student may present an opinion but struggle with the points supporting that opinion
Writing that is disorganized in terms of ideas	Production control (attention)	Weak planning often accompanies irregular use of outlining as a prewriting stage
Writing that does not contain extended thinking	Verbal elaboration (language)	Note whether the student's oral language is similarly sparse
Better capacity to recognize math procedures than to recall them	Long-term memory access	Recognition cues (such as a list of potential procedures) bypass long-term memory access
Particular difficulty with applying math procedures to novel situations	Conceptual understanding	Memory may be intact, but using procedures in new ways requires understanding them deeply
Trouble using reasoning and logic to discover a solution	Applied reasoning	Especially when the student cannot fall back on known procedures
Math diagrams that are more pictorial than schematic	Conceptual understanding	Schematic diagrams represent quantities and relationships; pictorial diagrams depict problem elements

while weaknesses in such areas as active working memory and attention production control can cause disorganized thinking (such as when writing) and time mismanagement (including planning long-term projects). When you encounter a student who is disorganized (and teachers encounter such students all the time), first clarify the nature of the disorganization (spaces and materials? thinking? both?). Then, by considering all that you know about the student from watching, listening, and looking at work samples, try to figure out what neurodevelopmental functions might be causing the disorganization. Identifying the underlying culprit will put you in a better position to select strategies that will help the student become more organized.

Here is one other thought about disorganization: avoid thinking of organization as a yes/no proposition. Instead of labeling a student as disorganized (or organized), consider the level or quality of organization. One possibility is to use a rating scale, with 1 being a total state of disarray and 10 representing impeccable organization. By looking at this issue as a continuum, you'll make setting progress goals for students seem more attainable. For example, it may seem daunting for a disorganized student to become organized, but the student, who would agree that he falls at 3 on the disorganization scale, may feel like he could work hard and get to 6, which would be enough to resolve a lot of his academic difficulty (say, with handing homework assignments in on time).

Bottom Line

Remember, this book may be used as a reference, so if you're feeling overwhelmed, realize that you don't need to absorb all of this information immediately in order to start helping struggling students. Bite off just what you can chew and, over time, integrate more pieces.

The next chapter is devoted to learning strategies based on students' neurodevelopmental profiles. Here are some additional thoughts about developing a deeper understanding of the learners in your classroom:

- Again, this process may seem like a lot to take on in addition to the myriad demands you face as an educator.
  The goal, though, should be to combine this approach with your existing knowledge and experience, and to incorporate this way of thinking into what you already do. With a little time and practice, looking for neurodevelopmental clues and using them to make instructional decisions will become second nature. So rather than being an add-on, this approach should represent a shift in your perspective.
- As should be evident from this chapter, you have an enormous amount of information at your disposal to help you understand your students. Also, be sure to meld information from the parents' perspective (such as what was discussed in Chapter One) to round out your picture of the student.
- Remind yourself always to look for strengths. Getting caught up in a search for answers about a student's weaknesses is very easy, but all students have assets and you can find just as many clues that reveal what a student can do as what he can't do.

4

Picking Strategies for the Classroom

THE INSIGHTS IN THE PREVIOUS CHAPTER FORM A ROAD MAP TO HELP you select learning strategies. If your school uses an RTI model to support students, you are now better equipped to pick strategies at any tier of service. This chapter describes such learning strategies, presenting them according to neurodevelopmental area (such as memory or language). Bear in mind, though, that the strategies discussed here are just the tip of the iceberg. Use them as templates to generate your own instructional tactics, to find strategies from other resources, or to repurpose techniques you already have in your professional toolbox.

Starting Pointers

1. *View these strategies as course corrections, not add-ons.* Being busy is a fact of life for educators. Now that you have a lens through which to interpret information you already have at your fingertips, you can use what you learn to make decisions about how you work with struggling learners. Strategies intended to help a single student can actually benefit many students (although perhaps in different ways). Also, investing time with an individual student will probably pay off later.

2. *Be willing to experiment.* Teaching is a continuous exercise in decision making: how to structure a unit, organize a lesson, pose a question, clarify a point, provide feedback, and so on. You make many of these decisions as educated guesses, and then see how things unfold. The kinds of strategies discussed here can be implemented in that same spirit of experimentation. You're selecting them on the basis of sound hypotheses, but give a strategy a shot even if you're skeptical, and then monitor how well it works.

3. *Be creative about making things fun as well as substantive.* Innovation is a cornerstone of good teaching, so innovate ways to make strategies as enjoyable as possible for students. Even seemingly boring drills can be cast as games, for example.

4. *Be creative about leveraging strengths and affinities.* You also should have a feel for a student's neurodevelopmental assets, so try to take advantage of those. For instance, good expressive language could be used to talk through new information and to bolster conceptual understanding. A student with a strong interest in cooking might better absorb procedural information by viewing it as recipes rather than as algorithms. Be sure to tell the student why you selected a strategy—how it addresses a weakness but taps into a strength or interest.

5. *Design tasks that reverse the input-output flow.* Many times the effective strategy is one that alters the direction in which the student usually works. For example, difficulty reading and setting up math problems (a form of input) might be addressed by having the student create word problems (an output exercise). Challenges with essay writing (output) could be tackled with proofreading challenges using text written by someone else (input). Reversing the current, so to speak, often gives the student insight into the skill or task involved by offering a new perspective.

6. *Carefully consider your objectives.* Priorities can get skewed whenever lessons or assignments address numerous objectives. If the assignment is to write a paragraph about how tornadoes form, how important are spelling and punctuation relative to factual retrieval, clarity of explanation, and critical thinking? This isn't to say that basics such as spelling are not important, but they don't need to be important all the time. Challenge your assumptions about priorities, because this will pave the way for the selective use of bypass strategies (also known as accommodations or modifications).

Strategies for Unreliable Attention

This book couldn't possibly cover all of the potential strategies for handling weak attention controls. What follows is a representative sample of what is possible, with an emphasis on themes.

Classroom Structures

A host of tactics related to classroom structures can support kids with unreliable attention. The basic idea is to create an environment that is more forgiving of attention weaknesses. Lining up the desks in rows, insisting that students stay in their seats for long stretches, and asking them just to listen or perform monotonous work would all be tough on anybody's attention controls but would invite disaster for a student with weak attention. Allowing for physical movement, such as letting kids work while standing or even walking around, can pay dividends. Periodically shifting from task to task, or altering something about a task, can really help a student whose focus span is stretched to the limit. Good crowd control tactics can also help, such as getting kids to line up or to gather materials individually or in small assigned groups rather than in a whole-group stampede.

I started my career as a teacher and learned a lot from a veteran physical education teacher who showed me how to manage very large groups of students (such as minimizing downtime, giving brief and numbered instructions, and assigning students to consistent groups that could be moved around in an orderly fashion). I translated what I saw in the gym to the science classroom, to huge benefit.

Another angle on classroom structure is degree of redundancy. If students have only one way to get important instructions (such as by listening to what you say) or only one way to hand in material (such as putting it in an assignment box), then kids with attention weaknesses will be more vulnerable to problems. Redundancy means that students have backup options at their disposal. In addition to homework instructions being presented orally, they are also prominently displayed somewhere in the classroom, written in a syllabus that each student and family has at home, or even available via e-mail message or Web site. Some students perform better with fewer hard copies and more digital formats, such as completing a paper at home and then e-mailing it as an attachment rather than shuttling a printed copy to school.

Peers are often untapped resources for helping a student with weak attention. Think about assigning an "attention buddy" (or comparable term) to help out with tasks such as recording homework instructions, placing materials in backpacks, and handing in assignments. Every student in the class might benefit from having such a partner, but you could make sure that the students with attention problems have partners who are especially good with the details.

Reward Systems

Reward systems can help with attention problems by reinforcing positive behaviors such as staying on task, developing a plan before getting into the work, and self-checking. Target behaviors should be specific and within the realm of what the student can control. Involve the student in deciding what the target behaviors should be, as well as in what the rewards should be. Rewards don't have to be tangible; they can be in the form of time (such as a few extra minutes to play a game) or status (for instance, earning a special role, such as class messenger for the week). Keep the system positive (rather than punishing or removing privileges for undesirable behavior or lack of target behavior), scale it so that there will be chances for both small and big victories, and fade the system gradually so that the improvements have staying power.

Students can also be enlisted to keep track of their behavior in order to build self-regulation. For example, a student could have his own chart at his desk and record a check for every five-minutes he stays on task. He could tally every time he jots down a thought rather than blurting it out in class. He might maintain a running score for the number of errors he flags and then fixes in his writing or math. Self-regulation can be combined with a reward system, and a student might earn extra points for tracking his own behaviors rather than having you track them.

Scaffolding

Related to promoting self-regulation, numerous tactics provide scaffolding to improve aspects of attention. For example, a student who struggles with maintaining focus and absorbing important details during a lecture or class discussion might really benefit from structured note-taking guides. Such guides could be little more than empty outlines that preview how many topics and subtopics will be covered. But guides could also be more overt in their scaffolding by telling the student what to listen for and record in his notes, for example, "The three types of levers" or "Five important facts about Mayan cities." (Guides might also include space for recording specific information, such as "Lever type 1:" "Lever type 2:" and so on; or "Fact 1 about Mayan cities:" "Fact 2 about Mayan cities," and so forth.) Additionally, scaffolding could be combined with positive reinforcement by granting bonus points for each important piece of information recorded in the notes. Listening and note taking could even be cast as a scavenger hunt for critical nuggets of information.

Students with unreliable attention often have trouble gleaning enough information from a text, even with good receptive language. Note-taking guides can also be used with reading, to coach students on what to read for and capture. Guides could be described to students as logs or fact journals. Active reading tactics in general can be very beneficial when attention is unsteady. The recurring theme with such tactics is that the student engages with the text rather than glossing over it. Some students need to be explicitly taught how to circle or underline important points, jot down margin notes and questions, connect ideas with arrows, and so on.

Highlighters can be counterproductive because their use can easily be very passive (and most educators are familiar with the sight of a page completely painted in yellow highlighter). To mitigate this effect and promote active reading of the text, coach students to use more than one color of highlighter, with each color corresponding to a type of information. For instance, blue could be used to highlight important terms, yellow to mark the definitions of terms, and green to call attention to explanations of processes. Whether using a pencil or highlighter (or both simultaneously, which would really promote engagement), students might be given a rule such as to mark no more than three important pieces of information per paragraph (or five per page, and so on) to keep them thinking about and prioritizing the material they're reading. Again, the use of active reading tactics may need to be reinforced with a reward system until such tactics become habits of mind.

Table 4.1 lists the strategies for unreliable attention covered in this section, along with corresponding attention components (mental energy, processing control, and production control).

Table 4.1 *Strategies for Unreliable Attention*

STRATEGIES	ATTENTION COMPONENT	COMMENTS
Give students ways to move around appropriately	Mental energy	Allowing students to stand at their desks is a simple but helpful tactic
Use transitions to refocus students	Processing control	Transitions can be from task to task or could involve alterations to a task (such as changing game rules)
Crowd control tactics	Processing control; Production control	Be mindful of how best to organize student activity and traffic in order to avoid trouble spots
Present information in multiple ways	Processing control	Redundancy helps information to sink in more deeply
Assign "attention buddies"	Processing control; Production control	Peers can help with staying on task and being organized
Reward positive behaviors such as staying on task, developing plans, and self-checking	Processing control; Production control	Target specific behaviors in the student's control; involve the student in creating the system

(Continued)

Table 4.1 *(Continued)*

STRATEGIES	ATTENTION COMPONENT	COMMENTS
Have the student keep track of his own behavior	Processing control; Production control	Such as how long he stays on task and avoids an impulse, or how often he finds and corrects errors
Structured note-taking guides	Mental energy; Processing control	Could positively reinforce filling in information or make using guides a game
Active reading tactics	Mental energy; Processing control	Promote engagement with the text by marking important points and jotting down margin notes
Color-coded highlighting	Mental energy; Processing control	Students use multiple highlighter colors, each corresponding to a type of information
Forced prioritization of reading notes	Processing control	Establish a rule such as only three pieces of information can be marked or highlighted per paragraph

Strategies for Memory Gaps

Teachers face big enough challenges getting students to learn essential content: what pi is and how to use it, the importance of the Nile to early civilization in Africa, the function of mitochondria, and so on. But on top of teaching content, teachers have another charge that is frequently left by the wayside: teaching students how to learn. One could argue, actually, that learning good techniques for memorizing is more important, in the long run, than knowing about pi, the Nile, and mitochondria. When left to their own devices, students all too often resort to rote memory. (How many times have we heard students describe their studying tactic as "going over it"?) Students who struggle with long-term memory storage, in particular, need coaching in how to memorize, and how to plan for memorizing.

Using Different Formats

Using multiple modalities can make a big difference in how effectively information is stored. Some students memorize best in a particular modality, such as using a visual format or through auditory channels (such as reading or listening); when this is the case, get information into the ideal format if it isn't already. For most other students, however, it helps to study material that is in multiple formats. When studying synapses, for example, terms and important facts should be captured in text as well as in labeled diagrams, but also possibly in a table (listing types of synaptic connections and neurotransmitters) or in a graphic organizer that displays connections between important aspects of the topic (see Figure 4.1). Video clips on a wide range of academic topics are accessible on the Internet. Providing material in all of these formats is probably unrealistic, but the goal should really be for students to create the materials on their own. They would need coaching and examples, of course, but then they would have the tactics to store information effectively.

Making Connections

Long-term memory is like a library, with books representing pieces of information, the process of placing books on stacks akin to long-term memory storage, and pulling needed books off the shelves analogous to long-term memory access. Ideally, a student's memory shares another similarity with a key feature of a library: systematic filing systems. An integral component of such filing systems is that books are tagged for multiple categories.

Synapses are connections between neurons, or between neurons and other kinds of cells. A single neuron may have several thousand synapses, although some have very few. Most synapses connect axons to dendrites, but there are other types as well, such as axon-to-cell-body, axon-to-axon, and dendrite-to-dendrite.

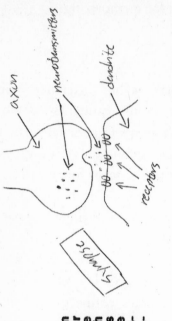

Figure 4.1 *Examples of Multiple Modalities*

So a book on Mercury belongs to such categories as planets, elements, mythology, and space flight pioneers. Filing books in multiple categories makes finding them easier. Similarly, pieces of information need to be interconnected during storage so that access is more efficient. The catch is that for students with memory gaps, such connections may not be obvious. Consequently, the teacher may need to make those connections as explicit as possible. For example, information about the Nile needs to be connected to information about the Amazon and Mississippi Rivers, irrigation systems, methods of transportation, and water deities. Every time such connections are illuminated, an important tactic for memorizing is modeled that students can eventually use on their own.

Recognition Questions

Free recall memory involves both long-term memory storage and access while recognition memory focuses on storage by providing prompts or cues for access. So recognition questions can be very beneficial for students who have stored information but have trouble accessing it on their own. Recognition question types include multiple choice, matching, and true-false. Most exams and quizzes need to contain some free recall items, such as fill-in-the-blank or open-ended questions, but a balance of question types might be struck.

Another possibility is starting with open-ended versions of questions and, if the student struggles, providing recognition versions of the same question, perhaps for fewer points. Also, the use of recognition questions does not have to be confined to written tests. Questions posed to a student with access problems during class discussion, for example, could be phrased to tap recognition. So instead of asking, "How do we calculate the area of a triangle?" one could ask, "Do we calculate area of a triangle by multiplying base and height, adding up the lengths of all three sides, or multiplying base and height and dividing by 2?"

Access Practice

Students with memory problems should spend plenty of time memorizing information in effective ways but also practicing how to access information. Too often, though, practicing access gets short shrift. As often as possible, give students opportunities to rehearse test-taking in low-stakes ways. For example, the last few minutes of class could be a test simulation, with just a few potential test items and questions given. This kind of practice can also mitigate test-taking anxiety. Students could also conduct such rehearsals at home, which may mean you'll need to help by making material available for this purpose (such as tests from previous years).

Finally, think about how important long-term memory is in the long term. Students memorize more during their school years than they will for the rest of their lives, but very few careers put a premium on memorizing. Much more important are reasoning, solving problems, building things, generating and critiquing ideas, collaborating, communicating, and so on. In the digital age of databases, wireless Internet access, and search engines, we have ready access to just about any fact we need—and most kids are very comfortable with these technologies. All this is not to say that we should forget about memory (no pun intended!) but that we should put it in this context. A student who has memory gaps needs to know that his future won't be derailed by his memory.

Working Memory

Two general approaches can be used to support students with limited active working memory. The first approach is to help students make the most of the working memory capacity they have through better use of strategies. The second approach is to minimize the effect of weak active working memory through accommodations. Some strategies may incorporate both of these approaches.

Chunking is a strategy that can help make active working memory more efficient. The basic idea is that working memory has a limited number of "slots" (7 is a number agreed upon by many experts). Adding slots is not really possible, but putting more information in slots is possible. Remembering a long series of digits (such as 9, 7, 8, 2, 4, 9, 2, 7, 5, 4) would be very difficult without chunking them (for example, 97, 82, 49, 27, 54; or 978, 249, 2754). Students can be coached to chunk not just numbers but also other kinds of information, such as procedural steps and word lists. Chunking may take the form of condensing information, for example, converting a procedure such as "Total the length of all sides to calculate the figure's perimeter" into something more compact such as "add sides."

Think about your social security number or telephone number. You probably don't recall such numbers as strings of individual digits. Rather, you access them as a small set of multidigit numbers.

Weak active working memory causes the most trouble when students have to do several things simultaneously. Taking some tasks off the student's plate, so to speak, can minimize the effects of limited working memory. Many things have to be mentally juggled when solving multistep math problems, for example, such as recall of math facts. Providing students with a reference for math facts, such as a multiplication grid (a 12-by-12 grid on which facts can be found by matching rows and columns) or a calculator, can spare working memory capacity for other tasks, such as executing a procedure or checking to see that the answer makes sense. Writing involves several simultaneous tasks, so students with weak working memory benefit from dividing the writing process in order to work on fewer things at once; for instance, a student may write a paragraph focusing only on word usage and grammar, and not worrying at all about punctuation or spelling. (Fixing such errors would come in a subsequent stage.) Reading also can be subdivided by requiring students to pause (or take a time-out) and answer questions frequently (such as after each section or even every paragraph) rather than at the end of a chapter; this way less information has to be juggled in active working memory during a given stretch of reading. Table 4.2 summarizes the strategies discussed in this section.

Table 4.2 *Strategies for Memory Gaps*

STRATEGIES	MEMORY COMPONENT	COMMENTS
Multiple modalities	Long-term memory storage	Students study or transform material using modalities such as diagrams, tables, and video
Illuminate connections between pieces of information and topics	Long-term memory storage	Some students need connections to be made more obvious; model how to make connections
Recognition questions, such as multiple choice	Long-term memory access	Recognition memory focuses on storage by providing prompts or cues for access
Rehearse accessing information	Long-term memory access	Rehearsal should simulate tests or quizzes but have lower stakes; students can rehearse at home
Coach chunking	Active working memory	Show how to put more information into available mental "slots," sometimes by condensing

STRATEGIES	MEMORY COMPONENT	COMMENTS
Provide references for math facts	Active working memory; Long-term memory access	Such as fact grids, number lines, and calculators; spares working memory capacity for other tasks
Separate writing tasks	Active working memory	Compartmentalize various writing components, such as vocabulary use, punctuation, and spelling
Require frequent time-outs when reading	Active working memory	Less information has to be juggled in active working memory during a given stretch of reading

Strategies for Limited Language

The previous section alluded to accommodations, which are strategies intended to bypass a weakness in some way. An example is having a student share information about the Great Wall of China in a bulleted list rather than in a traditional essay. In contrast, interventions are building strategies designed to improve a weakness. An example is providing a student with a skeleton outline to help organize information about the Great Wall, which is then used to write a rough draft and, after revising, a traditional essay. Students struggling with learning challenges such as limited language usually need a combination of strategy types—interventions for making improvements, accommodations for achieving particular objectives and experiencing some success. Deciding whether to use an intervention or accommodation often comes down to objectives. If the objective is to demonstrate knowledge of the Great Wall, for instance, then a bulleted list (or some other alternative to a traditional essay) might be acceptable. On the other hand, if the objective is to improve writing skill, then a skeleton outline (or other tactics designed to help with structuring an essay) would be the way to go.

Language Accommodations

When a student has limited language (receptive or expressive), a host of accommodations related to nonverbal information are possible. On the receptive side, provide the student with information that is conveyed visually or that is language-based material but with enough visual support to help the student understand it. This might mean providing more diagrams, models, video, or demonstrations than would normally be necessary, or placing more emphasis on the visual supports that are already available (such as walking through how to glean information from posters on the classroom walls).

On the expressive side, give students opportunities to utilize their memories and think with fewer demands on language. Another way to share knowledge about the Great Wall, for example, is to build a Web site or slideshow with a lot of images and effects (such as a series of maps displaying the Wall in different states over the centuries). Again, deciding whether to use interventions (such as strategies to improve reading comprehension or written expression) or accommodations will depend on objectives.

> Because the use of interventions and accommodations depends so much on objectives, make sure you devote sufficient time to clarifying objectives in your own mind. Break up routines, such as always having students write a report after reading a book when other ways of communicating analyses could do the job.

A critical barrier for many students with limited language is speed. Understanding language, even advanced material, may be possible given sufficient time. Similarly, verbally communicating sophisticated thoughts may be possible when not under time pressure. You probably have experienced these phenomena if you've ever studied a foreign language. When things are slowed down, comprehending and expressing are a lot easier.

> You may have noticed from the examples provided that some strategies are both accommodations and interventions.

One tactic for relieving time pressure is to provide students with advance warnings. For example, you might catch a student on the way into class and say, "Toward the middle of today's lecture I'm going to ask you to describe some of the reasons that the Panama Canal was built, so be ready for it." You've just primed the pump for this student, giving him time to ponder the question (which helps receptive language) and formulate a response (which addresses expressive language). Advance warnings don't necessarily need to be directed at an individual student; they could be displayed on the board or a screen or in a handout (for example, "You'll hear the following questions today, so be prepared to answer them").

> Advance warnings can also help students with long-term memory access issues, because they will have more time to retrieve information they have stored.

Advance warnings also help students with language limitations by kick-starting communication. You can provide scaffolding in several ways to get the ball rolling for a student, or provide a structure for more extended output. Sentence starters can be beneficial for younger students—for example, giving the first few words and then having the student complete the sentence. (Ending words or middle words could also be provided.) Similarly, the first sentence of a passage or paragraph could be given to older students. An outline would be a good kick-start for developing an essay or report; outlines can vary in terms of how much detail they contain, with the sparsest outlines merely displaying how to organize and sequence key points. A way to scaffold oral responses is to pose multiple-choice questions (rather than yes/no and open-ended questions). Giving students a few phrases from which to choose provides models for quality output and can initiate independent elaboration.

Language Interventions

Paraphrasing is a great way to develop language. To paraphrase something effectively, you have to understand it enough to distill the key points and then articulate those points clearly enough so that you will be understood. Students with limited language often struggle a lot with paraphrasing, but improving this particular skill can yield benefits in other aspects of language. The first step toward improving paraphrasing is to provide explicit coaching by, for example, posing and answering such questions as the following:

- When listening or reading, how do you decide the essentials to include in a paraphrase?
- How long should a paraphrase be?
- What are some tricks for organizing a paraphrase (such as numbering the key points)?
- What are some possible signs that your listener isn't following you?

Along with coaching, model effective paraphrasing and be transparent about what you're doing (such as saying, "Now I'm going to paraphrase by first describing the overall theme. Then I'm going to summarize the four main points, with a couple of details for each. Then I'll restate the major theme."). Practice with paraphrasing comes next, ideally in pairs or small groups so that students have smaller audiences. (Paraphrasing could be a homework assignment as well, with students required to paraphrase a topic for their parents or someone else at home.)

You can adjust the difficulty of the topic to be paraphrased by modifying such dimensions as length, complexity, and familiarity. Obviously, students with language challenges may need to begin practicing with material that is relatively short, simple, and connected to their experience and context. In fact, paraphrasing a topic related to the student's affinities may be a good place to start. A more advanced type of practice would be to have students periodically paraphrase information for the class, perhaps on a rotating basis so that everyone knows who will be paraphrasing next.

In a sense, expressive language is about building something out of smaller pieces. Word parts are used to build words. Words are used to build sentences. Sentences are used to build paragraphs. Paragraphs are used to build essays and stories. You can provide practice with the building process by putting various language parts on cards that students can then sequence. For example, you could put several prefixes, suffixes, and base words on cards that the student could then use to create as many words as possible. Individual words could be put on cards for the student to use to generate various sentences. Sentences (perhaps clipped from a newspaper article or short story) could be put on cards that the student could put in a logical order to make paragraphs. Finally, you could clip paragraphs from an extended piece of text and ask the student to string them together into coherent discourse. A student with limited language may not need all of these forms of building practice; select the versions that target a problematic aspect of language, such as semantics.

Finally, students with weak phonological processing often need intensive, systematic instruction in order to gain ground with their decoding and spelling skills. Several well-regarded approaches and programs are available for this purpose, including Orton-Gillingham, Lindamood-Bell, and Wilson Reading System. In addition to being sequenced and structured, such programs are often multisensory, meaning that practice with word sounds and written symbols occurs in several parallel channels: auditory, visual, even tactile (such as writing or tracing symbols in conjunction with hearing or enunciating sounds). Table 4.3 summarizes the strategies described in this section, including both accommodations and interventions.

Table 4.3 *Strategies for Limited Language*

STRATEGIES	LANGUAGE COMPONENT	COMMENTS
Present information in nonverbal formats	Receptive language	Figures, diagrams, pictures, and so on may augment language content
Allow students to communicate in nonverbal formats	Expressive language; Verbal elaboration	Examples include models, charts, and multimedia presentations
Provide additional time for comprehension and expression	Receptive language; Expressive language	Could take the form of a few extra moments during a discussion, or an extended deadline
Advance warnings	Receptive language; Expressive language	Gives time to ponder questions and prepare responses; also helps with long-term memory access
Sentence starters	Syntax	Provide a few words and have the student complete the sentence
Passage starters	Verbal elaboration	Provide the first sentence or outline and have the student complete the passage
Pose multiple-choice questions	Syntax; Verbal elaboration	Having a few phrases provides models for output and can facilitate independent elaboration

STRATEGIES	LANGUAGE COMPONENT	COMMENTS
Paraphrasing—coaching, modeling, practicing	Receptive language; Verbal elaboration	How to select essential details, appropriate length, organization, and checking in with listener
Word-building practice	Semantics	Put prefixes, suffixes, and base words on cards and have the student create words with them
Sentence-building practice	Syntax	Put individual words or phrases on cards and have the student create sentences with them
Passage-building practice	Verbal elaboration	Put sentences or paragraphs on cards and have the student create passages with them
Intensive, systematic instruction for decoding and spelling	Phonological processing	Quality programs typically are sequenced, structured, and provide multisensory instruction

Strategies for Weak Graphomotor Function

Weak graphomotor function can be improved, bypassed, or both, depending on the severity of the problem, the age of the student, the writing demands the student faces, and priorities. An elementary student with mild to moderate difficulty controlling a pencil would probably be a good candidate for explicit coaching in handwriting mechanics (possibly with an occupational therapist). This student likely would also benefit from supports around the classroom, such as diagrams illustrating letter formation, and graph paper to help with lining up letters and lines of text.

On the other hand, a middle school or high school student, especially one with moderate or severe graphomotor problems, would possibly be best served by eliminating as many handwriting demands as possible. This may mean allowing more assignments and tests to be typed on a computer for this student than for most other students (obviously keyboarding practice would need to be provided if necessary). Other ways to bypass graphomotor difficulty and allow the student to utilize other neurodevelopmental functions such as expressive language and long-term memory access include oral presentations, dictating and transcribing, and voice-recognition software. Students can communicate understanding and knowledge in ways other than a written or oral report, such as visual-spatial projects (for example, a model depicting the solar and lunar eclipses).

For a student with weak graphomotor function, note taking can be an arduous task. Providing a copy of lecture notes to the student would be the most substantial bypass strategy. Short of that, the student could be provided with an outline to fill in with details or key points. Also, coach how to take notes as concisely as possible. For example, "Zeus is the king of the Greek gods, the ruler of Mount Olympus, and the god of the sky and thunder" could be condensed for note taking as "Zeus—king of gods, Mt. Olympus, sky/thunder." It may not occur to students to take notes in this way and they may need practice to master it. When graphomotor function is a challenge, decreasing handwriting can make a big difference in productivity.

Strategies for Shaky Concepts and Reasoning

As a teacher you are constantly introducing new concepts to students, and many students will pick them up with little difficulty; but the student with weak conceptual understanding needs more overt support with concepts. One step you can take is to provide instruction, perhaps to all students, about what a concept is: a group of features (sometimes called critical features) that form an idea or category of ideas. The teaching of a concept (such as what a polygon is) is an opportunity to discuss the notion of concepts, especially if you use a consistent format when describing critical features (closed figure, made with straight lines, each line intersects exactly two others at each end), examples (triangle, rectangle, octagon), and nonexamples (circle, oval). Students could keep concept journals in which they list the names, critical features, examples, and nonexamples.

Connections are integral to concepts, and you will have to make connections more obvious for students with weak conceptual understanding than for most of your other students. Whether you're teaching about realism or dependent clauses or prime numbers, use multiple modalities and formats to describe how critical features connect to each other, and how concepts then connect to other concepts (such as realism to surrealism, dependent clauses to independent clauses, and prime numbers to composite numbers). You can connect by comparing and contrasting sets of critical features and examples and nonexamples.

When the reasoning process does not come naturally to a student, you may need to provide scaffolding in the form of a protocol. In other words, provide a blueprint that spells out the steps to take and in what order to take them when tackling a challenging problem. Blueprints may vary by type of problem or subject, but some consistent ingredients would probably include, first, clearly describing the problem, brainstorming potential options for a solution, evaluating options, and selecting and then implementing an option. After modeling how to use such a blueprint, you could provide practice using it—initially with scenarios that seem safer and more approachable to students than academic material, such as a student's affinity. For example, a student who is very interested in marine animals might practice a reasoning blueprint by solving an invented dilemma, such as how to help a pod of orca whales trapped in a harbor.

Talking About Learning

Having considered all of the clues about a student's learning at your disposal, you can now formulate a profile of strengths and weaknesses. The profile can then help you make choices about strategies, some of which were described in this chapter. One of the most important strategies, no matter what the student's profile includes, is to promote students' understanding of their strengths and weaknesses. Instilling such self-knowledge should be in the mission statement of every school, because life-long success with learning and work is greatly enhanced by knowing one's assets and challenges. When a student realizes what his profile is, he is likely to experience a boost in self-esteem, for two main reasons. First, his strengths may never have gotten so much emphasis before. Second, his weaknesses may never have been described with such specificity and concreteness (such as "limited active working memory space" or "shaky spatial ordering"), which can debunk negative thinking such as, "I'm no good at school" or "Everyone is smarter than me" or "I'm just an idiot."

You can also give a struggling student a shot in the arm by destigmatizing learning problems. Talk openly about the fact that everyone (really, *everyone*) has some sort of neurodevelopmental weakness. Some challenges are more visible than others, and challenges may emerge at different times. No brain is perfect! You can get this point across by describing your own weaknesses and how you deal with them. Also, promote optimism by praising specific successes; many small wins can add up to a huge victory.

Be sure to overtly connect the strategies you employ with what you know about the student's profile. So, if you implement a game to bolster phonological processing, for instance, the student should know why. With younger students you may need to substitute other terms or metaphors (such as "how your brain

hears little sounds inside words"). Ideally, discussion of neurodevelopmental functions will become part of the vernacular of
your classroom. Refer to the Atlas of Neurodevelopmental Terms
in Appendix Three for metaphors and explanations.

By being positive and transparent in how you talk about
learning and strategies, you can boost your students' morale,
confidence, and motivation to continue working on what might
be very challenging weaknesses.

Bottom Line

This chapter has presented a great deal of information that you
can refer to later as needed. Here are a few take-away ideas:

- Partner with parents at every opportunity, because strong
  home-school collaboration benefits struggling learners.
  When teachers and parents share an understanding of a
  student's profile, they are in a great position to brainstorm
  and invent strategies. Coordinated implementation of strategies can be very effective, because parents are often able to
  work on things at home, one-to-one, that may be difficult
  to do in the classroom.
- Partner with students at every opportunity. The student,
  even if he is young, should be an integral member of his
  own support team. The previous section described the
  importance of explaining the rationales behind the selection of strategies. You might be surprised at the ideas a
  student can contribute when he understands his profile
  and is given a chance to be heard.
- Think of new strategies as alterations to your instruction. Time is not a luxury in the teaching profession, so
  rather than finding more time, use your limited time more
  effectively.

- Embrace the challenge of teaching about learning, not just about content. Granted, many pieces of content are critically important for future study, career, and citizenship; but one could argue that the real value of much academic content is that it provides practice, that it can be used to enhance the ability to communicate, to reason, to store information, to create new material. Acknowledging this potential paves the way to the development of learners who have self-insight and the tools to succeed in any scenario.

PART

When More Help Is Needed

"Going into an assessment, I had speculated that my daughter had weak attention. But the team of specialists looked carefully and it actually turned out to be difficulty with spatial perception. That knowledge led us down a different, and more effective, path to success."

—PARENT

"Once the parent really understands what's going on with her child, everything else falls into place. There are reasons things are challenging; your child is not just doing things to make you crazy. When your kid sees that you get this, it takes a huge load off his shoulders."

—LEARNING SPECIALIST/SCHOOL PSYCHOLOGIST

5

Being a "Smart Shopper" for Educational Assessments

PARTS ONE AND TWO OF THIS BOOK HAVE EQUIPPED YOU AND YOUR child's teacher to discover and interpret clues about learning, and to use what you learn to make good choices about strategies to help your child. However, despite your best efforts and the efforts of your child's teacher, you may need to recruit the help of someone who specializes in learning problems. You may come to this realization as a parent (some reasons will be discussed later in this chapter), or the school may suggest an assessment in pursuit of special education services. In any event, the work that has been done to better understand your child has not been for naught; it will help guide you to find the right professional, jumpstart the assessment, and get the most out of the process. Put simply, now you can be a smarter shopper.

Although the chapters in Part Three of the book are written for the parents' perspective, the ideas and considerations certainly apply to educators as well.

Starting Pointers

1. *If and when the time comes to bring in an expert, think of it as consultation, not testing.* Put simply, you need answers, not just test scores. A good assessment of a student's learning often includes tests but should also incorporate a broad range of qualitative information, such as reviewing work samples and interviewing the student (to search for many of the same clues that were described in Chapters One and Three). The assessment process, however, should be a means to an end; ultimately the expert needs to interpret all of the gathered information so that you understand what's going on with your child and so that your child understands what's going on with himself. Then the expert should help you make decisions about learning strategies based on your child's profile (using the same kind of thinking described in Chapters Two and Four).

2. *Use recommendations from others, but ask for specifics.* You may know other parents who have had a child assessed for learning problems, or you could readily find such parents with whom to talk. Going on a recommendation for an expert is fine, but see what you can learn from others in order to make the best choice. Here are some basic questions you can ask as a smarter shopper:

- What did you like about this person?
- Was it just testing, or were a range of information sources considered?
- Were your observations and insights utilized?
- Did you come out of the process with a better understanding of your kid?
- How well were your questions answered about why your child struggles?
- Did you get good guidance about strategies and instruction?
- How did your kid feel about the process? Were his strengths identified along with any weaknesses?

3.   *Be willing to shop.* At this point you likely are feeling pressure and maybe even some desperation about getting your child some help. However, the adage about haste making waste often applies with learning assessments. This chapter can help you to make a decision about which expert to use, so do your best not to settle. Sometimes a parent has limited choices in an expert (due to few options in a small community or difficulty traveling to experts in other regions); but within your range of choices, bear in mind that you can walk away from an expert if you don't feel satisfied with the services provided.

When Is It Time for an Expert?

At this point you probably know more about learning than most people, and you certainly know a lot about your child; but someone might need the consultation of an expert for many reasons, including the following:

- Narrowing down possible explanations for learning difficulties
- Uncovering other possible explanations
- Getting a second opinion about your hypothesis
- Anchoring performance to age-based expectations
- Generating and prioritizing strategies
- Gaining a deeper understanding, for both you and your child

This section discusses these scenarios that might warrant getting an expert's viewpoint.

You may struggle with narrowing down the possible explanations for your child's learning difficulties. Chapter One presented numerous clues that you might uncover and what they could reveal about how your child learns. But sometimes learning problems can be complicated, with multiple factors converging to create difficulty. Also, in many situations potential causes of learning problems (such as active working memory and atten-tion production control) can be hard to differentiate. If you find yourself facing these kinds of dilemmas, an expert could help you to tease apart the possibilities and pinpoint the sources of difficulty.

You might have uncovered a factor in your child's learning struggles (such as phonological processing) and implemented some strategies accordingly (such as playing pig Latin) but not seen improvements after giving the strategies a chance to gain traction. Maybe something else is going on in addition to what you've discovered. Perhaps active working memory is con-spiring with phonological processing to make the decoding of long words difficult, for example. In any event, an expert can help you identify additional causes of your child's learning problem.

You may want a second opinion, perhaps because you are not comfortable with where your assessment process led. This may be the case, for example, if attention looks like the culprit. Many parents are anxious about attention issues because of the ADHD label and pressure to put kids on medication (which often is not necessary in order to manage attention weaknesses, by the way). So you might want an expert to take a closer look and weigh in on your hypotheses. The result could be a confirmation of your con-clusions or a different take on what's going on with your child.

An expert has the tools and experience to view your child's learning with age-based performance anchors. In Chapter One, one of the starting pointers was to find a basis for comparison for inter-preting the potential clues about your child's learning. The idea is that if you don't have benchmarks of some kind (such as how older siblings, or same-age friends and classmates, may have performed on similar tasks), knowing what is expected for a student your child's age may be hard. If you find yourself perplexed by how your kid should be doing for his age or grade, an expert can help.

You may need more strategies than have been provided in this book or that you have found on your own. Perhaps you've exhausted the options you've learned about—for example, spatial ordering—and need more; or maybe you've nailed down the underlying causes of your kid's learning struggles (such as semantics) and need an expert to help you decide which of the many possible strategies to prioritize. An expert will have a knowledge base of such strategies.

Finally, you simply may want to understand your child on a deeper level. If you've already utilized the information provided in this book, you likely know a great deal about his learning, but you may very well want to know more. An expert can provide that broader and deeper understanding but can also document the description in a written report that you can have for reference going forward and for sharing with others, such as teachers and tutors. In addition, you may want your child to understand better how he learns, particularly with regard to his strengths. Sometimes kids need to hear positive things from someone other than a parent.

Search Criteria: Picking the Right Expert

The education field includes several disciplines, each with a particular range of expertise and a perspective on learning. In addition, experts within each discipline differ in their particular training and experience. Table 5.1 contains descriptions of the major disciplines in the learning field, including common advantages and disadvantages (I use the term *common* because each professional is unique, so all of the points presented here may not apply with a given individual). Bear in mind that many professionals conduct assessments as teams; for example, a neuropsychologist may work in tandem with a learning specialist, allowing them to combine their advantages and make up for individual disadvantages.

Just as important, if not more so, as an expert's discipline, however, are the other qualities the person brings to the table. For example, you need someone who can think neurodevelopmentally,

Table 5.1 *Professional Disciplines in the Learning Field*

DISCIPLINE	DESCRIPTION	COMMON ADVANTAGES	COMMON DISADVANTAGES
School psychologist	Master's- or doctoral-level training in areas such as assessment, intervention (addressing challenges), and consultation (with parents and other professionals)	Well-versed in use of standardized achievement batteries, IQ tests, and other normed instruments; assigned to public schools, so have access to students, teachers, and classrooms	Heavy caseloads; often bound to prescribed batteries and methods of eligibility determination (for special education services); may have limited knowledge of interventions
Neuropsychologist	Doctoral-level training in the structure and function of the central nervous system; clinical neuropsychologists focus on the assessment and treatment of brain-based problems	Have a wide array of assessment techniques at their disposal; usually assess and describe students in terms of neurodevelopmental profiles	May not make clear connections between a profile and academic skills, which can limit explanations of learning breakdowns and recommendations of customized strategies
Clinical psychologist	Usually doctoral-level training in several areas, such as psychotherapy and assessment of emotional functioning	View assessment as a process of identifying symptoms and patterns that reveal underlying causes of a referral concern	Not associated with schools; little to no training in academic areas and learning strategies; may focus on making a diagnosis rather than on delineating a profile
Learning specialist	Usually master's-level training in academic assessment and strategies; also known as educational diagnostician, educational therapist, or psychometrician	Deep knowledge of academic skills, including potential breakdown points and strategies	Will not necessarily think in terms of neurodevelopmental profiles when describing students; assessment techniques usually limited to academics

DISCIPLINE	DESCRIPTION	COMMON ADVANTAGES	COMMON DISADVANTAGES
Speech-language pathologist	Usually master's-level training in assessment and treatment of speech and language problems	Have access to a variety of tools for assessing different aspects of language; assigned to public school systems, so have access to students, teachers, and classrooms	Heavy caseloads; may focus on treatment of speech and articulation rather than overall language; often bound to pre-scribed batteries and methods of eligibility determination
Behavioral-developmental pediatrician	Specialized training in behavior and learning issues (such as attention deficits) that can affect children	Can determine if learning challenges stem from a medical cause (such as insufficient sleep); can prescribe medication when warranted; provide long-term follow-up support	Not associated with schools; little to no training in academic areas and learning strategies; may focus on making a diagnosis rather than on delineating a profile

meaning they have knowledge of the neurodevelopmental functions described in this book. Surprisingly, not all experts are well-versed in, say, active working memory or syntax. Another key aspect of thinking neurodevelopmentally is the capacity to connect functions and skills. Don't take for granted that an expert knows about the role of phonological processing in spelling, for instance, or spatial ordering in math.

Training from All Kinds of Minds provides education professionals with knowledge of the neurodevelopmental framework and learning strategies, as well as the philosophy of thinking in terms of profiles rather than labels.

Obviously you need an expert with a knowledge base of learning strategies. No expert has every possible strategy memorized, but the well-prepared ones have the information readily available and know how to make good selections. Be wary of those who are so focused on the assessment process (or worse, on testing in and of itself) that they don't have sufficient ideas for how to support your child's learning.

Again, assessment should be about understanding. Even after an expert reveals a student's neurodevelopmental profile, the job is incomplete. Both you and your child need to find out what's going on with his learning, so you need someone who has good communication skills. A profile usually should be communicated in both written and oral formats. Consequently, the professional needs to write a clear report (the next section describes what to look for in such a report) and be able to talk to you and your kid so that you both understand.

To get a description of your child that promotes understanding, the expert will need to set aside diagnostic labels. If your child is struggling with reading, how helpful is it, really, to be told that he has a "reading disability" or a "reading disorder"? When you go to a physician with a throbbing headache, would you be satisfied to be told that you have a "headache disorder"? What you'd want to know is why your head hurts, and what to do about it. So you need someone who is not focused on labels so she can tell you, for example, why your child struggles with reading and what to do about it.

If the assessment is conducted in a public school, you need a professional who is not so focused on determining eligibility for special education services that your child's neurodevelopmental profile doesn't get revealed. One way of meeting legal requirements for special education is to compare a student's IQ to his scores on individually administered academic tests. This *discrepancy formula* is falling out of favor, fortunately, but you may still encounter school systems and experts who use it (see the Glossary of Testing Terms in Appendix Five for more information). Under such circumstances, you may need to use some of the questions in Table 5.2 to make sure you get what you need out of the assessment. Another possibility is that the school uses RTI as a way of organizing services and for identifying the level of support an individual student needs. With RTI, however, an understanding of a student's neurodevelopmental profile will help you make decisions about which strategies to implement, regardless of the tier or level of support. So again, use the questions provided here to ensure that the assessment process is beneficial.

An assessment should yield a full understanding of the learner, which means identifying strengths, not just weaknesses. Unfortunately, many experts become overly focused on students' learning problems, especially when driven by a search for a diagnostic label. Experts who use profiles to describe students are much more likely to search for strengths along with weaknesses, but even when they converge on a diagnostic label, they can illuminate strengths as well; they just need to be willing to do so.

Assessment should be a process of consultation. The point of asking an expert to learn more about your child's learning is to find strategies for better success. You need questions answered, not just in the here and now but over time. So you'll need an expert who is willing and able to provide ongoing follow-up. Every few months (or even more frequently, depending on the issues and situation), you'll probably need to talk to the expert, who can help you solve problems and act as a sounding board for your concerns. Ideally the professional would also meet with your child periodically, to reinforce his understanding of his strengths and weaknesses. Also, that person could provide follow-up directly with your child's teachers; this would be easier, obviously, if the expert worked at the school.

Finding an expert with all of the qualities described in this section may seem like a tall order, but they do exist. In addition, by being clear about what you want (such as a profile rather than a label), you can steer an assessment in the right direction. To find an expert who can really make a difference for your child, you'll probably have to probe a bit to get a sense of what kind of assessment you would get. Table 5.2 lists potential questions to use when looking for an expert; think of these questions as mini-scripts for being a smarter shopper.

What Makes a Good Written Report?

A tangible product you'll be getting from a learning assessment is a written report, which will document your child's strengths and weaknesses, the evidence for both, and the strategies to be used to help him succeed. If you were to hire a carpenter or painter you would probably want to see their other projects to judge the quality of their work. In the same vein, you should ask to see an example of a report the expert has written. To protect confidentiality, names and personally identifying information would need to be removed; many experts have model reports on hand for this purpose.

With a sample report in hand, how do you judge how well it would suit your needs? Here are some features you need, at a minimum:

- *Descriptions of strengths.* Assessments should illuminate strengths, and reports should convey important information about them, including how they can be better utilized to create successful experiences for the student.
- *Prioritization of weaknesses.* In some instances a student may have just a handful of weaknesses; but when a student has multiple weaknesses, the expert needs to prioritize them so

Table 5.2 *Potential Questions to Use When Looking for an Expert*

QUESTION	WHAT YOU'RE PROBING FOR
What framework do you use to understand and describe the learning process of students?	Capacity to think neurodevelopmentally, not just in terms of diagnostic labels and eligibility criteria; whether the assessment will produce a descriptive profile
Given that my child is struggling with [insert academic area], what are the major potential root causes of such a difficulty?	Knowledge of the possible connections between neurodevelopmental functions and academic skills; willingness to dig deep for answers about underlying causes of a learning problem
How do you select strategies for the unique needs of a student? What are your sources?	Depth of knowledge related to learning strategies (interventions and accommodations); capacity to use a student's profile to craft a personalized plan for success
What tactics do you use to explain a student's learning profile to him?	Quality of oral communication skills; how well the expert can connect with your child so that he comes out of the process with a better understanding of his learning strengths and weaknesses
May I see a sample report you have written?	Quality of written communication skills; creativity with different methods to convey findings in a report, such as diagrams and metaphors (rather than all text and test scores)
After you've collected and analyzed the findings, will you pull everything together into a profile of strengths and weaknesses or into a diagnostic label?	Predisposition toward describing a student with a unique profile rather than simplifying learning issues with a diagnostic label
If you are going to use a prescribed set of tests to determine eligibility for special education, how are you going to look beyond scores to understand my child's profile?	Capacity to go beyond requirements and mandated procedures; willingness to explore possibilities and provide insights that will help your child succeed; predisposition toward describing a student with a unique profile

(Continued)

Table 5.2 *(Continued)*

QUESTION	WHAT YOU'RE PROBING FOR
Please give me some examples of how you have incorporated students' strengths into their learning plans.	Outlook on the importance of strengths in terms of identifying them through the assessment and then leveraging and nurturing them to improve success
What sort of follow-up services can we expect after the assessment?	Availability and willingness to collaborate with you, school personnel, and your child to reinforce understanding of the child's profile and how to implement strategies

that you know which ones to tackle first; how to set priorities is part of the expertise an expert should bring to the table.

- *Answers to referral questions.* The expert should explain in the report what's going on with your child; for example, if a student struggles with decoding, the report should describe why (without resorting to a diagnostic label).
- *Customized learning plan.* Look for a report that includes strategies that connect with the specific needs of the student; for example, if math is problematic, the strategies would differ if the underlying issue is conceptual understanding rather than long-term memory.

Ideally a report should have some other qualities, but be forewarned: unfortunately, few experts in the field write reports with the following features:

- *Clear explanations of jargon.* Technical terms (such as *phonological processing*) can be hard for an expert to avoid in reports, and such terms do provide a common vocabulary for other experts and educators; best practice, however, is to explain jargon, possibly with a metaphor (such as likening long-term memory to the book shelves in a library).

- *Visual communication.* Although text may be the dominant format for conveying findings and describing a profile, creative experts communicate with other techniques, such as diagrams and figures; even breaking up text into shorter sections with clear subheadings can help, as can bolding and italicizing terms and key phrases.
- *Integration of information types.* Assessments should always include information that is qualitative (such as descriptions of how a student solved a problem, not just whether he got the answer right) to go along with quantitative scores; the best reports provide clear explanations of both qualitative and quantitative findings.

> The Glossary of Testing Terms in Appendix Five explains terminology you may encounter in assessment reports, including types of scores.

Finally, here are some red flags to watch for when reviewing a sample report (by the way, just because you see features like these doesn't mean you necessarily have to avoid that particular expert; she may be willing to change the report format or content if you clarify at the outset what you want, or don't want):

- Extensive list of weaknesses without priorities
- Little to no discussion of strengths
- Unexplained list of test scores
- Focus on diagnostic labels
- Boilerplate learning plan

The report you get from the expert will be one of your most important tools for helping your child. Also, it will tell part of your child's life story. So make sure you know up front what kind of report you would be getting.

You Get What You Ask For:
Effective Referral Questions

A referral question (also called a referral concern) is simply what you would want the expert to address in the assessment. It's what you're worried about as a parent. Often parents have multiple referral questions. By asking specific, clear referral questions, you can increase the odds of getting the most out of the assessment process (the topic of the next chapter), but the posing of referral questions is also an aspect of being a smarter shopper. Referral questions communicate what you need, and prospective experts' responses announce whether they have the knowledge, experience, and willingness to dig deep for answers that can help you and your child.

Referral questions should be as specific as possible. One way to achieve specificity is to zero in on a particular academic skill. For example, asking, "Why does my daughter have so much trouble with reading?" is much more specific than, "Why does she have trouble with schoolwork?" But an even more specific question might be, "Why does she have trouble decoding words?" You can also be specific by mentioning a potential cause, such as, "Could weak phonological processing be behind her decoding trouble?" So asking a referral question is a chance for you to share what you've learned about your child's learning from your own observations. Don't hesitate to use the terminology you've learned from this book, because it shows that you want specific neurodevelopmental explanations.

You're not going to be satisfied with an answer to a referral question that uses a label. For example, responses to a question about trouble with decoding such as, "Because she has a reading disability" or "She has dyslexia" won't deepen your understanding or help you select strategies. So, along with posing specific questions about what you want to know, you may also have to clarify that you are not interested in diagnostic labels. Also, if you introduce the idea that multiple culprits might be at work (for example, "What are the factors behind my son's inaccurate spelling?"), you'll also communicate that you're not looking for the singular, simplistic explanations that labels provide.

In summary, good referral questions

- are as specific as possible, such as by zeroing in on an academic skill breakdown
- include a hypothesis (if you have one) about what's causing the breakdown
- don't mention a diagnostic label (such as dyslexia or ADHD)
- introduce the possibility that multiple causes might be at work

Table 5.3 lists some potential referral questions, one for each of the neurodevelopmental areas and one for each major academic skill. This is not an exhaustive list. Again, you've probably learned a lot about your child by this point, and that knowledge can help you generate your own questions. View the questions listed here as templates. You'll notice that several questions tap multiple areas of concern, which is OK. Learning is complicated; a neurodevelopmental function can feed into several academic skills, and all academic skills are influenced by multiple functions. By posing a question that includes such complications further indicates that you want specificity and clarity, not a simplistic label.

Bottom Line

Here are some headlines about being a smarter shopper when looking for an expert to help you understand your child's learning:

- A learning assessment really should be a consultation. You're at this point because your child is struggling and you need answers, so you need an expert who will collaborate with you to chart a path toward more success.

Table 5.3 *Potential Referral Questions to Pose to an Expert*

AREA OF CONCERN	QUESTION
Attention	Is my son's attention processing control unreliable, or is it just that he loses focus because he doesn't understand due to weak receptive language?
Memory	My daughter struggles with recall of information. Does she have a long-term storage problem, long-term access problem, or both?
Language	Language seems to be problematic for him—but what specific parts or levels of language?
Spatial ordering	He seems to have trouble with visual material. How significant a problem is it and how could it affect his schoolwork—including upcoming grades?
Graphomotor function	Her handwriting is barely legible to me. How off-target is it for her age and what could be done about it?
Conceptual understanding	Does my son have a core issue with grasping concepts?
Applied reasoning	Could shaky reasoning be the culprit behind her math and science challenges?
Reading decoding	What's undermining his decoding of words?
Reading comprehension	Why does she have so much trouble understanding what she reads?
Spelling	Why is my son's spelling more accurate with isolated words than when he's writing a paragraph?
Writing	What are the causes of my daughter's writing problems?
Math operations	I have a feeling that long-term memory is behind his math calculation errors. What do you think is going on?
Math reasoning	When my daughter gets lost during a math problem, does she not understand the concepts or does information slip out of her active working memory? Or both?
Information literacy	He gets really confused and frustrated when conducting online searches for his schoolwork. Would you please figure out why?

- A diagnostic label or set of test scores won't provide the answers you need. Labels are too global and simplistic to be of benefit when selecting strategies. Test scores in and of themselves don't provide insight. You need interpretation of findings and clear explanations.
- Be sure you'll be getting a thorough description of strengths and weaknesses, answers to your specific referral questions, and useful recommendations.

6

Getting the Most Out of the Assessment Process

THE TIPS IN THE PREVIOUS CHAPTER CAN HELP YOU FIND SOMEONE who can guide you toward a better understanding of your child's learning, but being a smarter shopper is not enough. You also need to be a smart customer and do everything you can to maximize the investment you're making in your child's success.

The logistics of an assessment may vary. For example, some experts see kids in a clinic as part of a team, some see them in a school setting. Some will devote a whole day to your child, some will schedule multiple shorter sessions. Regardless of how an assessment is conducted, you can take some simple steps to enable you to learn what you need to do to help your child.

Starting Pointers

1. *Share information.* Assessing learning problems is a challenging process, even for experts. To do it well, a lot of information needs to be gathered and analyzed. What you know about your child's learning is just as valuable as what the expert discovers during testing. So think of yourself as a partner in the assessment. When you share information, be as specific as you can (for

example, "His writing doesn't have very many interesting words" is better than, "He doesn't write well").

2. *Ask questions.* Questions are probably the best tools for getting a good assessment. Obviously you can ask questions to learn more about the assessment process and about your child, but you can also use questions to steer the expert's thinking in more productive directions; this will be covered in the section called "Head Off Simplification" provided later in this chapter.

3. *Remember that you need insights and answers, not labels and jargon.* Hopefully your selection process has put you with an expert who will describe your child and provide explanations rather than rely on a diagnostic label, but if you start hearing jargon, ask for it to be explained. If you start hearing labels (such as learning disability or ADHD), say that what you really want is a description of your child's strengths and weaknesses. Don't be a passive recipient of services. Be willing to stand up for yourself, and for your child.

Share What You Know

You know a lot. You're seeking the support of an expert in order to learn even more and to help you make sense of what you already know. Experts have deep knowledge about learning in general, education issues, and how kids develop; but you have expertise about your child. You'll get a helpful assessment if you can combine your expertise with that of the clinician. Look at it this way: in order for clinicians to do the best job, they need a lot of information, just like detectives working to solve a mystery need plenty of clues.

A clinician may ask you to share information in a few ways. Many ask parents to complete a questionnaire before the clinician meets with the student. The items on the questionnaire might be multiple choice with a scale of some sort (such as, "How well does your child remember math facts? *Very well, OK, Struggles a bit, Has great difficulty*"). These kinds of items allow the clinician to review a lot of information relatively quickly and to look for patterns (such as a lot of items related to memory checked as "*Has great difficulty*"). Questionnaires could also contain open-ended questions (such as "How is your child doing with math?") that give you more of an opportunity to describe what's been happening and what your concerns are. Responses to open-ended questions usually require more time to review, but they can be rich in insights. Many questionnaires contain a balance of item types. The clinician might also ask your child's teacher or teachers, and even your child, to complete a questionnaire.

Clinicians often use interviews to gather information, so someone might spend some time asking you questions about your child's learning. The professional discipline of the expert will dictate the kinds of questions you'll get, to a certain degree. For instance, a speech-language pathologist will likely focus on such issues as early vocabulary development whereas a pediatrician will want to cover more medical history and a psychologist would probably screen for any emotional difficulties that might accompany learning problems. Setting these professional differences aside, you can expect some core questions (that mostly will be open-ended) such as when you first became concerned about your child's learning (and why) and what steps you've already taken to address your concerns (and what has resulted from those steps).

> Your child should also be interviewed as part of the assessment process, with such questions as, "What is your favorite part of school?" or "What is the hardest subject for you?" The interview questions may be interspersed throughout the testing session or sessions.

Whether you are responding to open-ended questions on a questionnaire or during an interview, you can help the expert glean the most information by following a few basic guidelines. First, share what you have observed firsthand, because that is information that no one else can provide. Comment on what you have seen during homework time or what you have noticed in work samples. You'll probably also need to share secondhand information, such as what teachers may have told you about what happens in the classroom; this is fine, but just clarify the source. Here is a list of guidelines for sharing information:

- *Be specific in your comments.* The most revealing information zeroes in on the issue; get as specific as you can, pulling from the various sources of information you learned about in Chapter One; consider these examples of comments that range from vague to very specific and informative.
  - *Vague:* "My son is having huge problems at school."
  - *More specific:* "My son is really struggling with math and with writing."
  - *Very specific and most useful:* "My son can't seem to remember much about math, such as facts or how to solve problems; and he forgets all sorts of things about writing, such as where to put commas."
- *Use examples (but don't overuse them).* Examples can clarify the points you need to share about your child; for example, "They're learning fractions right now and he can't seem to keep straight how to add and subtract them" is a great illustration of memory difficulty in math; just be mindful of generating laundry lists of examples, because they can get you entrenched in a topic or subject at the expense of considering other angles.
- *Cover several academic areas, even those that might be going well for your child.* Math and writing, for example, may be your

big worries at the moment, but to really understand what might be going on in those areas, the expert will likely need to know about reading and other skills and subjects; looking across the board can help reveal specific breakdown points but just as important, can illuminate assets as well.

- *Emphasize recent history.* Share history, but know that the most current information is generally the most relevant; in other words, focus on the here and now. Information about your child's early years, for example, may be revealing in some cases (for instance, language problems often show up as delayed vocabulary development during preschool); but the likelihood is that what's happening now will yield the most useful insights about your child.

- *Keep the focus on your child.* Without intending to, parents sometimes let their comments drift to other topics, such as siblings (especially to make comparisons) and their own learning issues.

- *Be mindful of venting.* You may be experiencing a range of negative emotions, such as worry or frustration, and you have every right to feel them; a valid reason for seeking an expert's help is to alleviate such feelings. The assessment process will offer opportunities for you to vent about your child (such as how often she forgets her homework materials); just try to keep tabs on how much time you spend blowing off steam, so you can help the expert learn as much as possible about your child.

Head Off Simplification

If you didn't already know it before picking up this book, you probably appreciate now just how complex learning problems are. One of the reasons you're seeking help is that your child is complicated. Every once in a while the explanation for a learning challenge is relatively straightforward. For example, weak active working memory can wreak havoc in all academic areas, but you and your child will be ill-served by rash convergence on an explanation (and a diagnostic label isn't much of an explanation). You want the expert to consider all the evidence before drawing conclusions. This section provides techniques to help you head off simplification of your child's learning issues.

Name Some Suspects

You can use referral questions to set the stage for thinking beyond the simple explanation of labels. Chapter Five described how referral questions can help you identify the best expert to help your child. Referral questions also are opportunities to share your hypotheses about your child's learning problems. Put differently, referral questions are like suspects you have identified in your detective work. They may not pan out, but they can prompt the expert to think outside the box of easy answers.

To review, here are the tips about referral questions that were discussed in Chapter Five:

- Be as specific as possible.
- Share any hypotheses you have about what's causing breakdowns.
- Don't mention a diagnostic label (such as learning disability or ADHD).
- Introduce the very real possibility that multiple factors might be at work.

Table 6.1 is designed to help you generate good referral questions. The first column contains questions aimed at academic areas. You can use these if you don't have specific hypotheses; they will still be useful because they are phrased to focus on a

Table 6.1 *Referral Questions Based on Academic Skills*

WITHOUT HYPOTHESES	WITH HYPOTHESES
What are the factors behind his trouble with *reading decoding*?	Could weak *phonological processing* be behind his trouble with phonics for decoding? She has such a hard time matching letters and sounds. Could *long-term memory* be a factor?
Why does she struggle with *reading comprehension*?	Is it possible that she doesn't understand reading because weak *attention* prevents her from absorbing enough detail? Is her reading comprehension difficulty part of a larger challenge with *receptive language*? Because word definitions really trip him up, could *semantics* be at the core of his weak reading comprehension? Could *syntax* be undermining her understanding of reading, causing confusion at the sentence level? I'm wondering whether he just can't hold enough information in his *active working memory* when reading.
What are the reasons for his inaccurate *spelling*?	Might weak *phonological processing* be undermining his phonics for spelling? She has such a hard time matching letters and sounds. Could *long-term memory* be a factor? Could *active working memory* be affecting his spelling, such as when he has to spell a word in the middle of a passage?
What are the causes of her *writing* problems?	Does he not get enough down on paper because of shaky pencil control? Is this a *graphomotor* problem? Is her writing difficulty part of a larger challenge with *expressive language*? Because word definitions really trip him up, could *semantics* be at the core of his weak written expression?

(Continued)

Table 6.1 *(Continued)*

WITHOUT HYPOTHESES	WITH HYPOTHESES
	Could *syntax* be undermining her writing, causing confusion about how to structure sentences?
	Does her sparse writing reflect a more general language difficulty with *verbal elaboration*, with extending thoughts?
	Writing just exhausts him. Might *attention* be the culprit? Might he have insufficient *mental energy*?
	Is it possible that she is a disorganized writer because weak *attention* hinders her planning and quality control?
	Maybe he just can't juggle all of the task components for writing in his *active working memory*.
What's undermining his *math operations*?	Does he have a problem with *storing* math information in his *long-term memory*?
	Does she have trouble *accessing* math information from her *long-term memory*?
	Could he be getting lost in the middle of calculations due to weak *active working memory*?
	Is she having a hard time with the visual aspects of math due to weak *spatial ordering*?
Why is *math reasoning* so difficult? Please help us uncover the reasons.	Is it possible that she makes math mistakes because weak *attention* prevents her from picking up important details?
	Could math be a struggle because weak *attention* hampers his planning and quality control?
	Does she get confused by math word problems because of a larger challenge with *receptive language*?
	Because word definitions trip her up, could *semantics* be at the core of his math difficulty?
	Could *syntax* be undermining his understanding of word problems, causing confusion at the sentence level?

WITHOUT HYPOTHESES	WITH HYPOTHESES
	Is he struggling with the nonverbal aspects of math due to weak *spatial ordering*?
	Does he not "get" math ideas because of shaky *conceptual understanding*?
	We're wondering how well she can use her *applied reasoning* to think through math problems.

particular skill, they don't mention diagnostic labels (such as dyslexia), and they may raise the prospect of several underlying factors. The second column includes additional questions for each academic area, this time containing hypotheses. The work you have already done to understand your child's learning problems can steer you to ask some of these questions (which are like a line-up of usual suspects).

The referral questions in Table 6.1 are all structured around academic skill areas. You can also ask questions that start with neurodevelopmental functions. If you have hypotheses about a function that you think might be affecting several skill areas at once, you might want to pose questions like those in Table 6.2.

When Labels Rear Their Heads

Labels aren't very helpful when it comes to understanding learners deeply. In fact, they can even be harmful in that they may promote close-minded and defeatist thinking about a child—sometimes even creating self-fulfilling prophecies. If you're fortunate, your selection process has connected you with a clinician who will not use labels to describe your child. Also, you can state at the outset that you're not interested in labels, but what should you do if, despite your efforts at prevention, you find your child getting labeled?

Table 6.2 *Referral Questions Based on Neurodevelopmental Functions*

Mental energy (attention)	How much brain fuel does she have for schoolwork, and how reliable is her fuel supply?
Processing control (attention)	Is my son's attention processing control unreliable, leading to difficulties with avoiding distractions and absorbing details?
Production control (attention)	How is her attention affecting school-work in terms of planning, resisting impulses, working at the right speed, and self-checking?
Active working memory	How well can he juggle information and mental tasks in his active working memory?
Long-term memory storage	My daughter struggles with remembering information. Does she have a specific problem with storing it in her memory banks?
Long-term memory access	Is it possible that he stores information in his long-term memory but has a hard time accessing it when he needs it?
Receptive language	Does my child have a general difficulty with understanding language, whether listening or reading?
Expressive language	Does my child have a general difficulty with generating language, whether speaking or writing?
Phonological processing (language)	Could weak phonological processing be behind his trouble with word sounds when decoding and spelling?
Semantics (language)	Does he have a specific language problem with semantics or vocabulary?
Syntax (language)	Is she experiencing particular language difficulty at the syntax or sentence level?
Verbal elaboration (language)	What's going on with his capacity to communicate extended ideas with language? How significant is his verbal elaboration challenge?

Spatial ordering	He seems to have trouble with visual material. How significant a problem is it and how might it affect his school-work?
Graphomotor function	His handwriting is not very legible. How off-target is his graphomotor function and what should be done about it?
Conceptual understanding	Does my daughter have a core issue with grasping concepts?
Applied reasoning	Could shaky applied reasoning be the culprit behind her difficulty solving problems and thinking things through?

Why would a clinician insist on labeling despite a parent's wishes? A clinician may do this with good intentions, such as wanting to find a portal into specialized services, at school or elsewhere. But even if a label can overcome gate-keeping obstacles, it shouldn't trump the importance of thoroughly describing strengths and weaknesses.

Your first course of action should probably be to reassert your desire for a detailed description of your child rather than a label. Here is a script that can be used as is or adapted depending on the circumstances:

We're not on the same page here, so I have to emphasize that what I really want and need from this process is a thorough description of my son's strengths and weaknesses—not a label. I want him to better understand how his mind works. We also need specifics about strengths and weaknesses in order to make good decisions about his instruction and learning strategies.

That opening phrase, "We're not on the same page here," will probably really grab the clinician's attention, which would be a good thing in this situation. It's a way of saying, "We're just not communicating." Experts generally aren't used to being challenged in any way, but that definitely doesn't mean they are above being challenged. You have every right to make your intentions clear so that your needs (and your child's needs) are met. When the clinician hears your wishes again, hopefully she will then veer away from labels and get back to revealing your child's profile; but if the clinician persists in labeling, your next course of action could be to pose questions or make statements to facilitate deeper thinking about your child's learning. Table 6.3 contains several such questions and statements, including the rationale for each (to give you a sense of when you might want to use them).

Table 6.3 *Statements and Questions for Heading Off Labeling*

STATEMENT OR QUESTION	RATIONALE
How does my child differ from other kids with the same diagnosis you're suggesting?	Labels such as learning disability or dyslexia are umbrella terms; but even under an umbrella term, students show significant diversity. This question is a reminder to consider that diversity.
Please list my child's specific strengths and weaknesses along with that label.	Ten students who meet the criteria for a label could still have ten unique profiles. This request will help the expert view your child as an individual, not just as a label.
How would this label benefit my child? How would it make him more successful with learning?	Given the harm a label can cause by pigeonholing a child, using a label had better have a huge upside. This question pushes the expert to make that case.
What would this label mean in terms of instruction and the strategies we should be using?	A huge benefit to getting a profile of strengths and weaknesses is that it will help teachers make decisions about instruction. Asking this question brings that need front and center.

STATEMENT OR QUESTION	RATIONALE
I understand that you have information that's steering you toward that label. Please describe the evidence that doesn't support that label.	Even experienced and well-meaning experts can fall into the trap of prematurely locking onto a diagnosis. This statement can help to remove blinders and let them see other possibilities.
What were the unexpected findings?	Asking about unexpected findings is another way to prompt the expert to consider other possibilities besides the label in question. Unexpected findings often contradict the evidence for a label.
Could the symptoms of ADHD that you've identified be caused by something else? Such as a glitch in language or memory, for example?	This is a more overt way to get the expert to think beyond a label. You could substitute any label or diagnosis for ADHD in this question.
Could something else be going on here in addition to the diagnosis you're suggesting? Could multiple factors be at work?	The intent of this question is to raise the possibility that your child's learning problems are more complicated than can be captured in a label.

You may have gotten a sense from observing your child that attention can be challenging to assess. One reason this is so is something referred to as a *secondary attention deficit*. Think about what life would be like if you lived in a foreign country where you spoke little of the language. Because you wouldn't understand much of what you heard, your mind would probably wander and as a result you would appear unfocused. Because you would have a hard time expressing yourself, you might do things to get your needs met that would appear disorganized or impulsive. This scenario is a metaphor for a secondary attention deficit stemming from weak language. A student could appear to have weak attention due to some observed symptoms, but the deeper (or primary) deficit is in language. Weaknesses in other areas, such as memory or graphomotor function, can also give the false impression that attention is problematic. Because secondary attention deficits are so sneaky, you may need to pose some questions to keep them from arising in the assessment of your child. Table 6.3 includes such a question specific to ADHD that probes for other potential causes of observed symptoms.

So, attention could be identified as a culprit when really it's not; but the opposite problem could arise, with attention being the primary cause of some other secondary deficits. Asking "How did weak attention affect the assessment results?" will help the clinician to consider whether other identified problems, such as weak language or memory, might actually be secondary to attention. For example, maybe your child struggled on tests designed to assess active working memory because of problems with attention processing controls and his active working memory is just fine. Put differently, attention often is a real problem, and when it is, you need to understand the full extent of it.

When labels rear their heads your general strategy is to get the clinician to avoid thinking in terms of a narrow diagnosis. You can make use of what you have learned from this book to get the expert to take off the blinders, so to speak. For example, if the expert brings up the label "disorder of written expression," ask about all of the potential causes of a writing problem. What about expressive language? Could graphomotor function be hampering your kid's writing? Is limited active working memory at the heart of the matter? Labels are obvious, easy, and unhelpful answers. Probing the full range of underlying factors can push the expert to consider all the possibilities.

Finally, if the clinician keeps emphasizing a label despite your stated wishes and attempts to broaden his thinking, you may just have to cut your losses and seek help elsewhere.

Observing the Assessment

Observing the assessment can help you get the most out of the process for a couple of reasons. First, *by watching your child during testing, interviewing, and so on, you'll learn even more about his strengths and weaknesses.* Even though you'll likely get a written report that conveys the findings (and the expert may also meet with you to explain the results), by observing firsthand you'll be able to connect the dots more easily. For example, you may read in a report that your child struggled with memorizing a word list that was presented several times but his attention seemed to be getting in the way of his memory. If you had observed the assessment you could think back to what you saw and recall how your son did seem distracted during that task, much as he seems to lose focus when doing his homework.

Second, *observing the assessment puts you in a position to contribute to it.* Any testing situation is inherently artificial. Your child usually works in your home or in a classroom, not in a clinical setting. You can compare your child's behavior to what you usually see in the natural settings and let the expert know whether the testing situation itself is a significant factor in the results. You can also fill in some gaps for the expert. For instance, you may see your daughter jump right into a task involving the assembly of blocks to form a design, much like she often impulsively starts her work with little forethought; sharing such an observation with the expert would highlight the importance of her approach to the block assembly task and validate the results. Later in this section you'll find a list of pointers for observing the assessment that includes ways to share the most useful input.

How might observing the assessment work from a logistical standpoint? Many clinics have assessment and observation rooms separated by one-way mirrors. Some clinics are outfitted with cameras and microphones so you can watch and listen on a remote monitor. Either setup allows you to observe without being in the same room, which minimizes the potential distraction of your close proximity. If a team is assessing your child, one expert might speak with you while another works with your child. Another way to observe is for you to be in the same room with your child. This arrangement has its drawbacks, obviously, but also some advantages. For example, a skillful clinician might take advantage of your presence by asking you questions along the way, to get your real-time input about how your child works and learns. Your only option may be to sit in the same room if the assessment takes place in the school (the usual protocol for school psychologists). You should know that school-based clinicians generally don't have parents observe the assessment, but not because it isn't possible. You are within your rights to make such a request, which may require special arrangements to accommodate (such as finding a big-enough testing room). If you get resistance, just communicate how important observing is to you and why.

Perhaps surprisingly, students are rarely bothered by being observed during an assessment. On a rare occasion a student (usually a teenager) may feel so self-conscious that different arrangements need to be made. But by and large kids are fine with parents watching and listening.

So what should you do while observing the assessment? Have paper and pencil on hand so that you can take plenty of notes. You'll want to record thoughts to share with the expert, questions to ask the expert when you have the opportunity, and notes that will help you recall what you saw later, such as when you read the report. Here is a list of pointers about what to look for, ponder, and ask about during the assessment.

- *Gather examples* of tasks, questions, and answers to help you and your child understand the findings; when the expert shares with you a finding (such as that your child is good with semantics), you can then link back to moments when your child used interesting words or provided detailed definitions; you may need to ask the expert to make those links.

- *Keep a running list of procedures and tests* that were used; ideally the clinician will provide some sort of guide to explain the tests, including what skills or functions they assess; if not, take note of the procedures so that you can ask about them later; for instance, record the kinds of questions (such as asking for word definitions) or tasks (such as drawing an abstract figure from memory) and not necessarily the test names.

- *Collect burning questions* for the expert to answer for you; watching your child will likely spur several of these (such as "Why did he answer the question that way?" or "What was the significance of her approaching the task like that?").

- *Compare your child's behavior* in the assessment to what you normally see; think about how the context might account for differences (fewer distractions in the testing situation? more one-on-one attention from an adult?).

- *Look beyond the accuracy of answers* and take note of such things as confidence, motivation, and enthusiasm. You know best how to read your child's emotions (such as the way she acts when she's feeling nervous); try to discern whether confidence or motivation fluctuates and why (perhaps in relation to particular subjects or tasks). Emotions are often clues for revealing strengths or weaknesses, because we naturally feel positive when we're successful and negative when we're struggling.

Finally, what should you do if you can't observe? First, you should realize that the assessment can still be a valuable process for you and your child. Second, you can pose some of the same questions you would have asked had you seen the assessment. Inquire about your child's demeanor and behavior in order to get a sense of how he responded to the testing situation. Ask the expert if your child did or said anything that requires some explanation. Perhaps she made a comment that needs your clarification or validation. Maybe she approached a task in a particular way and the expert needs to know whether that is your daughter's usual method. Posing questions has the benefit of cuing the expert to consider information beyond test scores and ponder what occurred during the assessment session. Posing questions also helps to establish you as a contributor to the process, not just a recipient of information and advice.

Bottom Line

During the assessment, keep reminding yourself why you have embarked on this process: to get a better understanding of how to help your child have more success with learning. The point of assessment isn't to get test scores or a diagnostic label or special education eligibility. If you keep a firm grasp on the goal of deepening your understanding, you will be in a better place to keep the assessment on track.

- The assessment shouldn't just provide *you* with a better understanding; your child also needs to emerge from the process knowing more about his learning strengths and weaknesses.
- Be willing to push the expert to provide clear explanations. If you're confused about something (or you sense your child is confused), ask for clarification (or an example or metaphor).
- You are your child's most important advocate. No one will have a more significant role than you in setting the stage for more learning success. So push yourself to thoroughly understand the assessment process and the findings.

- Be an active participant in the assessment process by
  - sharing the information you've gathered on your own
  - communicating what you think may be going on with your child
  - posing good questions to the clinician to help frame the assessment and ensure that your child is thoroughly understood
  - observing the assessment, if possible

7

Using What You've Learned from the Assessment

So what happens once the assessment is over? Keep in mind that the goal of the assessment was to gain a deeper understanding of your child's learning so that you and others can make better decisions about strategies and instructional approaches. Now that you have that understanding, you need to share it and put it to use. The assessment is not the finish line; it should mark the beginning of a new era for you and your child.

Starting Pointers

1. *Continue to help your child understand her learning profile.* The expert needs to share the assessment findings with your child in a way that is understandable, specific, honest, and hopeful. Strengths should be given as much, if not more, airtime as weaknesses. You need to keep reinforcing those messages.

2. *Seek the support you need to navigate paths to success.* The expert who conducted the assessment should be an ongoing resource for you. Knowing your child's strengths and weaknesses will be a big help, but you're going to have plenty of questions as

your child advances to higher grades, changes schools, and faces new academic demands. So tap that expert through follow-up contacts.

3. *Keep tabs on your child's progress.* Supporting your child's learning is a long-term process. Following up with the expert can also help you track how your child is doing. This kind of follow-up might take the form of a reassessment, or it might involve just answering some questions so that the expert gets a sense of where things stand.

Keeping Your Sights on Insights

Again, you and your child are embarked on a long journey. An important part of keeping that journey on a positive trajectory is helping your child learn about learning. Self-knowledge about learning and thinking is referred to as *metacognition,* which also encompasses knowledge about learning in general. Continually educating your child about his strengths and weaknesses, and about how they affect learning, will develop metacognition. Also, having regular discussions can remind you what life is like for your child. For example, talking about your son's limited active working memory underscores for you both how much a toll it takes on math and writing; he doesn't avoid those tasks or come up short due to lack of effort or motivation, but rather because he has such a hard time juggling information in his head.

Where and When to Discuss Profiles

The assessment process should conclude with the expert sitting down with you and your child for a discussion of the findings. This kind of conversation goes by different names, including *interpretive session* and *debriefing.* The findings should be shared so that your child, regardless of age, gains insight into her learning. The expert should provide a thorough description of strengths and affinities, a targeted list of specific weaknesses (not labels, such as ADHD, but neurodevelopmental functions, such as phonological processing), and explanations for how those strengths and weaknesses affect schoolwork. For example, good expressive language could be the reason your daughter is so good at sharing ideas during class discussions, but weak graphomotor function makes getting those same ideas down on paper very hard.

Dr. Mel Levine uses the term *demystification* for "taking the mystery out of learning" by providing insights about a profile as well as about learning processes in general.

As powerful as such a discussion may have been for your child, and for you, the effects will fade unless you find ways to reinforce the important messages on a regular basis. Sitting down with your child and reviewing everything the expert covered is probably not realistic, and may not even be desirable. Rather, find ways to sprinkle message points into the many interactions you have with your child. Regularly hearing about a strength or weakness in relation to natural contexts (such as doing homework or studying) will give those ideas more authenticity and traction.

So the key is to find teachable moments, or openings to discuss aspects of learning. Such opportunities arise on a daily basis during schoolwork and life in general. Remembering how a student's profile connects to academic skills will help identify openings. For example, knowing the neurodevelopmental functions involved with spelling paves the way to discussing phonological processing and long-term memory when a student is practicing how to spell words. Table 7.1 lists some examples of

Table 7.1 *Examples of Teachable Moments About Learning*

SCENARIO	WHAT COULD BE DISCUSSED
Practicing decoding skills, such as how to attack lengthy words	The importance of listening carefully for word sounds (phonological processing); word sounds have to be matched with letters (long-term memory)
Reading a novel, short story, or textbook chapter	Understanding text requires receptive language, but also attention to detail (processing control) and juggling pieces of information (active working memory)
Composing a story with a pen or pencil	Words and sentences come from expressive language but have to be sent like signals to hands and fingers for writing (graphomotor function)
Composing a book report using a computer	Good writing takes planning and self-checking (production control), a lot of brain fuel (mental energy), and juggling of multiple tasks (active working memory)
Completing a math assignment	Procedures have to be stored in and accessed from long-term memory; solving problems requires carefully thinking them through (applied reasoning)

these kinds of teachable moments and includes academic skills and related functions (refer to the Glossary of Academic Skills in Appendix Four for more details). Remember that teachable moments should involve both strengths and weaknesses so that you can talk about skills and functions even when things are going well.

The examples in Table 7.1 stem from academic work, which means they apply to educators as well as parents. For teachers, being transparent about neurodevelopmental functions can benefit all students in the classroom. When students are practicing oral presentations, for instance, talk about the importance of expressive language. Describe the need for processing control (to filter irrelevant details) during online research. Discuss how spatial ordering is important for constructing diagrams or models. Because such functions underlie all academic skills and tasks, the possibilities are too numerous to list.

Teachable moments arise all the time in the context of learning strategies, such as those described in Chapters Two and Four. For example, if you set up a scavenger hunt (in which the student earns points for identifying the important details in a textbook reading assignment), talk about how the game will strengthen her attention processing control. When coaching a student to take notes using graphic organizers (or cluster diagrams), discuss how his good spatial ordering is being leveraged to bolster his long-term memory storage. When practicing how to summarize a story, describe how the activity relates to expressive language. Explaining the rationale behind strategies also helps students buy into the process.

Parents also have opportunities to reinforce messages about learning outside of academic work. One example is organizing around the house and the need for spatial ordering (to plan the best use of space) and processing control (to weed out irrelevant materials). The next section includes additional examples, along with more details about what to discuss. Finally, look for times to talk about learning that are relatively low-key, such as when you're in the car, during dinner, or when tucking your child into bed. The idea is to engage your child when he is more at ease and, hopefully, more willing to discuss challenges.

How to Discuss Profiles

Perhaps the most important tip about discussing profiles with students is to be straightforward and share what the assessment process revealed. Students need to hear about their strengths, including aspects of their profile that might be on-target for their age (as opposed to advanced) and that might be relative strengths (compared to their weaknesses). Bear in mind that students who have learning problems often have blind spots when it comes to their assets, because weaknesses have a way of dominating a school experience. So work to erase that blind spot by describing assets in a detailed way. Think about how much more powerful a compliment with specifics is (for example, "These pancakes you made are perfectly cooked—crispy outside and fluffy inside—and I love the cinnamon you added to the batter") than one that is generic ("Good job on these pancakes"). Bolster discussion of learning assets in the same manner, for example, "Your long-term memory is so great! I can't believe how well you remember details from that book you read last summer, and you've got your math facts down pat." Affinities can be folded into conversation about assets by talking about how amazing and important a strong interest is. For example, "You really love horses and you know so much about them—different kinds of horses, where they come from, how they've been used. You definitely know more about horses than I do!"

Here are more examples of statements related to a student's learning strengths. You can use them as scripts, modifying them as needed for the student and situation:

- "You have many more strengths than weaknesses."
- "Your strengths are far more important, now and in the long run, than your weaknesses."
- "Your strengths are amazing, and we're going to come up with ways for you to let them shine even brighter."

Be straightforward about weaknesses as well. Students should hear about prioritized specific weaknesses (such as phonological processing or long-term memory) rather than global labels (such as learning disability). Numbering the weaknesses puts boundaries around them and helps the student see that his shortcomings are finite. As much as possible, use neurodevelopmental terminology (such as *active working memory*). By using such terminology, you send the message that the difficulty has been identified by the field and that others have experienced it, which can be comforting. (Think about how unsettling it would be if a physician couldn't come up with a name, such as psoriasis, for an ailment your child was experiencing, such as a persistent skin rash.) Of course, with younger students you may need to find alternative terms. Metaphors can help with this (such as "your brain's gas tank" rather than "mental energy"); check the Atlas of Neurodevelopmental Terms in Appendix Three for such metaphors. If you use alternative terms, just make sure to use them consistently (don't switch metaphors, for example) to avoid confusion.

> Limiting the number of weaknesses to discuss with a kid to three is a good practice. Addressing more than three areas with strategies is very difficult anyway. Also, strive to counterbalance the weaknesses with an even longer list of strengths and affinities.

Here are some model statements for discussing weaknesses. Again, think of them as brief scripts that may be adapted for the child and situation:

- "There are three learning areas that we want to improve. First, . . ."
- "Even your weaker areas work OK sometimes. We just need them to be more reliable, more consistent."
- "We'll find strategies to improve or for getting around your weaker areas so that they don't get in the way of your strengths."

In addition to learning about their strengths and weaknesses, kids need to understand how those strengths and weaknesses affect their learning and schoolwork. For example, explain that weak active working memory derails math work despite good conceptual understanding and applied reasoning. Metaphors can also help explain such connections, such as describing how the student's laser beam (attention processing control) isn't zeroing in on the little details in textbooks and math problems. Connections between neurodevelopmental functions and academic skills are covered in Chapters One through Four, as well as in Appendix Three.

Here are some statements that could be used when explaining how a student's profile connects to academics:

- "Because your attention production control is unreliable, it isn't natural for you to plan out before you get started with homework."
- "Your active working memory has a hard time juggling all the little tasks of writing, such as spelling and punctuating and coming up with ideas."
- "Storing info in your long-term memory is no problem, which is why you can recognize right answers on multiple-choice questions. But you have trouble pulling that info out of your memory if you don't get much of a cue, such as a fill-in-the-blank."
- "Your brain's interpreter is doing a great job when you read or listen, but your brain's translator struggles to get words out when you have something to say or write."
- "Now that we know so much more about how you learn, we can make better choices about strategies for you."

You don't have to cover the whole learning profile every time you discuss learning. Talk about what makes sense in the moment, such as phonological processing during spelling or graphomotor function when handwriting. Both parents and educators can discuss learning beyond the particulars of a child's profile. Educators have countless opportunities to explain neurodevelopmental connections, such as when introducing a lesson or activity. Transparency about neurodevelopmental demands helps with teaching the hidden curriculum of learning about learning and preparing students to be independent learners beyond their school experience. Following are some statements that illustrate how to introduce neurodevelopmental ideas:

- "Let's practice solving math problems in our heads, so we'll need to juggle info in our active working memories."
- "Take a look at the diagram on page 77. You'll need to use your spatial ordering to make sense of it."
- "We're going to flex our conceptual understanding muscles by exploring a new idea called *photosynthesis*."
- "Your expressive language is going to be key for developing your class presentation."

Parents also have many chances to be transparent about neurodevelopmental functions and life skills. Again, you may need to substitute some alternative terms with younger students or those with significant receptive language weaknesses. You might be surprised, though, with how much terminology a kid can pick up, so you could start with the real names and use alternatives if necessary. Here are some examples:

- "There's no way my long-term memory can keep track of all the food we need this week, so I'm going to make a grocery list."
- "It's important that I use my processing control when balancing our checkbook, otherwise I'd make all sorts of little mistakes with our money."
- "I need to use my receptive language when I call for directions, or else I won't understand how to get there."

- "Let's use our spatial ordering to figure out where we are on this map."
- "We can try to solve the mystery in this book by using our applied reasoning."

Another way to discuss profiles is to talk about others who have experienced learning challenges but have still found paths to success. Many renowned and accomplished people fall into this category—more than can be named here (you can find lists on the Internet) but including Orville and Wilbur Wright, for example. Try to pick people with whom your child is familiar or with whom you think he could connect in some way, perhaps because of a similar profile or interest. For example, a kid who loves to invent things might be encouraged to know that perhaps the most famous inventor of all, Thomas Edison, struggled with learning.

Finally, kids can benefit from knowing about learning challenges that their parents faced (or continue to face). All too often, kids and parents share similar difficulties. If you find that to be the case, talk openly about your own experience—your frustrations and disappointments. Describe what worked for you or how things improved over time. Strive for empathy rather than preaching, or put differently, steer clear of "if I can do it you can do it" tones. Discuss specific moments of challenge, such as when you had a hard time preparing for a big test, getting a paper written, or learning certain math concepts. So many kids with learning problems feel defeated and alone. Hearing about a parent's struggles can help forge stronger alliances about academic work.

Navigating Paths to Success

Supporting your child through learning challenges is a long-term project. You shouldn't *feel* alone in your journey, and you certainly shouldn't *be* alone. The learning expert who assessed your child can be an important ally who can help you navigate your journey in many ways.

First and foremost, tap that expert for guidance in strategy selection. Decisions about strategies should be based on your child's learning profile, using the same thought process that was described in Chapters Two and Four. Make sure that you also get ideas for how to utilize your child's assets and affinities. For example, an affinity for space exploration could be leveraged by getting a student to read or solve math practice problems that have outer space themes. Ask the expert to brainstorm possibilities with you or with your child's teachers.

Contextual variables are also important when selecting strategies and instructional approaches. Ideally the expert will think about issues such as the number of students in a class, the experience level of the teacher, or how frenzied homework time can be. If you get suggestions for strategies that don't seem realistic to you, however, talk to the expert about your concern. Strategies can be adjusted to be a better fit for the situation, or they can be replaced altogether with other strategies. The expert also can reiterate the rationale and importance of a strategy, so that even if an idea seems like it will be a real challenge to implement, at least you'll know it may be worth the struggle.

Beyond strategy selection, a learning expert can help with the numerous other decisions you'll face on your journey. Some decisions (such as school changes) have bigger implications than others (such as which course a student should take), but all are significant. Issues on which you may need to consult an expert include extracurricular activities (type and frequency), summer camps, and tutoring (see the next section).

Finding a Good Tutor (If You Need One)

Why should a student have a tutor in the first place? Sometimes students need more instructional time than they are getting at school, or the instruction needs to be more intensive or specialized. Many students need help with organization, and a tutor can help kids with materials and task completion. But in many instances the main rationale for having a tutor is to defuse family tension. Although some parents and children get along just fine in the context of homework, others are like oil and water. Maybe the parent and the child aren't a good match in temperament. Perhaps the child doesn't like having his academic weaknesses exposed in such close proximity to Mom or Dad. Watching a child struggle, up close and personal, can be troubling and anxiety provoking for parents, which compromises the capacity for patience and calm thinking.

Identifying the reason or reasons for having a tutor is the first step in finding a good one. If the main need is specialized instruction, then you need to find specialized knowledge, experience, and training. Approach your search with an employer's mindset. The position you are filling has required qualifications that you can use to screen applicants. Knowing your child's profile (such as a math difficulty due to weak conceptual understanding) might give you enough information to list those qualifications, but you may need to consult the learning expert about this. Some tutors specialize in helping with organization. Many actually refer to themselves as organizational coaches.

You can find tutors in the Yellow Pages or online, but you may need to interview them to learn their qualifications. You can also advertise or get recommendations from other parents or teachers. Finally, the expert who assessed your child might have some names.

A tutor's professional skills are important, but so are other traits, such as open-mindedness, flexibility, creativity, and patience. Your child needs someone who can make use of what was learned through the assessment process rather than rigidly follow his or her own protocol. At the same time, though, you don't want a tutor who will get stuck in what might have been written in the assessment report; rather, the tutor needs to be inventive in crafting strategies that will best fit your child's profile and needs. Ideally a tutor can help your child continually learn about her strengths and weaknesses; this can be accomplished through transparency about strategies (such as saying, "Let's start off these math problems by circling all the key details to strengthen your attention processing control"). So, you may need to find out how well the tutor can think neurodevelopmentally, by asking such questions as, "What tactics will you use to bolster my daughter's receptive language?" or "What would help my son's writing difficulty given his weak active working memory?"

If defusing family tension is a major goal, then the tutor's temperament becomes a more important consideration. Negative family dynamics about homework often leave kids feeling discouraged and resistant about getting help from anybody. To counter such a pessimistic outlook, you may need someone with a calm demeanor and reserves of patience who can be especially positive and supportive of your child.

During the search process a prospective tutor could look very good on paper, come highly recommended, or even interview well, but still not work out for your child's needs. A tutor's temperament may turn out to be a mismatch for your child. A tutor may push your child too hard, or not hard enough. Perhaps the academic demands facing your child will change, evolving beyond the tutor's skill set. For all these reasons you may need to shift gears and find a different tutor.

How should you explain to your child the need for a tutor? First of all, take advantage of the opportunity to reinforce important messages about your child's learning—his strengths and weaknesses, and how those strengths and weaknesses connect with schoolwork. Then talk about how you're looking for ways to support your child so that schoolwork isn't such a burden (and is maybe even more fun). You might draw a parallel to an athlete needing a coach, a musician needing some specialized practice, an actor needing more rehearsal, or a political leader needing a consultant. Even the most accomplished, talented people seek support from time to time. Talk about how you have sought such help, either as a student or in life beyond school.

Keeping Tabs

You need to track your child's progress, and a learning expert can help you do this through the follow-up process. Again, learning experts should provide support for you and your child beyond the assessment itself; you can also tap them as consultants and advocates over the long term. The degree of the expert's involvement in tracking progress can vary from relatively informal check-ins (such as the expert talking with you about how things are going) to more formal and rigorous reevaluations.

Full-fledged reevaluations usually occur at intervals of at least two years. Going through the full assessment process more frequently than that usually brings diminished returns in terms of insights. Learning strategies and specialized instruction require time for improvements to be seen. Also, many of the assessment instruments that clinicians use are normed such that students should not see the items more than once every six months in order to mitigate against practice effects. A scaled-down assessment, using just some of the techniques from the original assessment, can be useful in tracking progress and requires much less time.

Regardless of the frequency or form of the reevaluation, here are some important areas to address:

- *Assets.* How are the previously identified strengths holding up and have any others emerged?
- *Weaknesses.* What is the status of weaknesses? Have they improved, stabilized, or gotten worse? Have other weaknesses emerged?
- *Connections to schoolwork.* How are strengths and weaknesses matching up with current academic demands, which are likely different than during the previous assessment?
- *Strategies.* Given the current state of the profile and considering academic demands, which previously used strategies should be abandoned or modified, and what new ones should be considered?

Three years is a standard reevaluation interval for schools while some specialized programs use a one-year interval for tracking individual student progress.

A reevaluation, or any kind of progress monitoring, is an opportunity to speak with your child about his strengths and weaknesses, and about how they affect the child's schoolwork. Your child definitely needs to know about any changes in his profile and should be aware of evolving academic demands.

Intelligence tests are commonly used for learning assessments, though there are trends away from such instruments. Such tests yield the most well-known standard score, the IQ. Other frequently used standardized measures are achievement or academic tests. See the Glossary of Testing Terms in Appendix Five for more information.

Learning experts may use standardized instruments during reevaluations, generating some standard scores in the process. Many parents are alarmed if they see score slippage on the same tests as were used in the previous assessment. A drop in a standard score does not mean that a student has gone backward or "unlearned" information. Understanding why this is the case requires some basic knowledge of normed scores. One step in the development of a standardized test is to administer it to hundreds, or even thousands, of students who represent a sample of the students for whom the test is intended. This sampling should take into account such factors as geography, socioeconomic class, gender, ethnicity, age, grade, and so on. No one factor should be significantly over- or underrepresented in the sample.

The scores of the students in the sampling are subdivided by age (and for some tests by grade as well). A mean score is then determined for each of these groups (such as all the eight-year-olds). These mean scores are the basis for determining the standard scores for the students who later take the test (such as a math achievement test). For example, when an eight-year-old takes that math achievement test during an assessment, the number of points he earns (such as from correct responses or time bonuses) is compared to the mean score of the other eight-year-olds in the original norming sample. If he performed better than most of those other eight-year-olds, his standard score will be high (above average).

But let's extend this example to include a reevaluation. Two years have passed since the initial assessment (Time 1) and our eight-year-old is now a ten-year-old. His performance during the reevaluation (Time 2) on the same math achievement test will be compared to the original sampling of ten-year-olds. At Time 1 he earned more points than most of the other eight-year-olds, yielding an above-average score. Let's say, though, that at Time 2 he earns more points than he did at Time 1 but about the same number of points as the original sampling of ten-year-olds. That would mean his Time 2 standard score would be in the average range and lower than his Time 1 *standard score*.

Does the fact that his Time 2 standard score is lower than his Time 1 standard score mean that his math skills have eroded or that he's forgotten math information? Definitely not. In the two years between Time 1 and Time 2 he has continued to learn math skills and accumulate knowledge; remember, he actually earned more points at Time 2 than at Time 1. At Time 2, though, his performance was pretty close to the mean score of all the ten-year-olds in the original sampling, whereas his performance at Time 1 was stronger than most of the eight-year-olds in the sampling. In essence, standard scores are comparison scores, because the student's test performance is compared to that of students the same age who were in the norming sample. (Refer to the Glossary of Testing Terms in Appendix Five for more information about standard scores and tests.)

Bottom Line

Even the most talented, experienced clinician is seldom a savior. A learning expert can provide insight and be an important source of support and guidance. But even though he may have a better road map in hand, the journey still belongs to you. You have work ahead, and so does your child.

- Don't let what you learned from the assessment grow stale. Keep using the findings and insights to navigate some challenging terrain.
- Keep in mind that the learning plan shouldn't be a document etched in stone. Rather, the plan should be dynamic and evolving.
- When you feel at a loss about how to help your child, return to the assessment findings and recommendations for guidance. This can help to

- ° get you back inside your child's head, to remind yourself what life is like for him
- ° stir your thinking about strategies, because the ideas the expert provided can serve as inspiration for other strategies

CONCLUSION

Brady and Cetera are the second graders introduced in this book's opening pages. Both struggle with reading and spelling, but for very different reasons. Brady's weak phonological processing undermines his capacity to interpret and manipulate small word sounds, so when he is reading he often drops word sounds (such as reading *winter* as *witter*), and when he is spelling he inserts extra letters (such as spelling *class* as *caless*). In contrast, Cetera's phonological processing is fine, but she has trouble connecting word sounds with letters in her long-term memory. So Cetera has particular trouble reading and spelling words with unusual sound-symbol pairs (such as *bridge*, which she might read as *BRID-gee* or spell as *brij*).

Fortunately for Brady and Cetera, their parents and teachers decided that just calling them dyslexic (because they certainly have trouble reading) or getting them labeled with a learning disability (and they may very well meet the diagnostic criteria) wouldn't do much good. Instead, they worked to figure out why Brady and Cetera struggle. They looked for clues, such as what kinds of errors they make when reading or spelling. Some clues the parents found on their own and some came from the teachers. They then put those clues together into patterns that revealed Brady's weak phonological processing and Cetera's shaky long-term memory for sound-symbol pairs. This better understanding helped them make decisions about how to support Brady and Cetera.

Knowing about Brady's phonological processing directed them to such strategies as word modification ("Change the /b/ in 'boat' to /k/. What word do you have then?") to help him improve how well he hears subtle word sounds and how he can alter those sounds. As a result, Brady improved his segmenting and reblending of word sounds when decoding and spelling. Cetera's parents and teachers were able to target her sound-symbol connections with such approaches as multisensory phonics instruction; while hearing a word sound (such as /f/), she was shown different letters that can represent that sound (*f, ph,* and *gh,* for example), wrote those letters on a small chalkboard, traced the letters in a sand tray, touched felt cutouts of them, and so on. She then improved her decoding and spelling accuracy as well.

Just as important, however, as the reading and spelling skill gains that Brady and Cetera made was how their outlook on school changed for the better, starting with a better understanding of their own learning. Their parents and teachers repeatedly described their strengths and explained the specific reasons for their learning struggles. They likened Brady's phonological processing to a walkie-talkie in his brain that wasn't getting clear signals about word sounds; his strategies were aimed at boosting power to his "word sound walkie-talkie." They depicted Cetera's long-term memory as a bookshelf of sound-letter pairs; her strategies were about putting more and more books on her shelf so that she could use them later when figuring out how to read and spell words. Brady and Cetera began to see that their struggles weren't the result of being "stupid" (as Cetera had once put it in frustration), that they had strengths, and that they could improve in their weak areas. They even started to mention their weak areas (in terms of a walkie-talkie and a bookshelf) as they engaged in strategies and improved in reading and spelling. For instance, Brady said, "My 'walkie-talkie' is picking up that sound better now!"

Things to Let Go Of

Helping students like Brady and Cetera find success is a real challenge—a long and winding journey. As with any journey, the odds of reaching the destination are improved if you pack the right things and leave at home what you don't need. This section describes some of the excess baggage best left behind.

In the opening chapter I mentioned how important it is to focus on the here and now, to let go of searches for causes of neurodevelopmental weaknesses (such as a child's experiences during infancy). You want to know what's beneath the surface of a child's academic skills (such as decoding or spelling), but rarely will you need to know what's beneath the surface of a child's neurodevelopmental functions (such as phonological processing or long-term memory). You may have noticed that this book has made no reference to brain anatomy. Although knowing about brain functions is important, parents and educators can sidestep thinking about where those functions exist in the brain. Brady's parents, for example, don't need to know which brain lobe accounts for his phonological processing in order to improve that function.

Devin was a thirteen-year-old who struggled not only academically but also emotionally. His parents worried about his self-esteem and his somber demeanor. After learning about his profile he realized he wasn't "an idiot," that he had strengths after all, and that by approaching his work differently he could be more successful. His mother described him as a new kid—one who has to work hard and still struggles from time to time but is so much more confident and optimistic.

Parents and educators alike have all sorts of expectations for kids, most of which are appropriate and positive; but be mindful of expectations that are out of step with the uniqueness of a student. For example, a parent may expect a certain level of organization that works for the parent rather than what is realistic or workable for the child. A parent or teacher may want a student to complete a task the same way the parent or teacher would do it or the way most other students would do it rather than think about an approach that meshes with the student's profile. Parents of older students may even plan out their kid's young adulthood (such as college, major, or even career) without realizing the extent to which they are making decisions. Mismatched expectations can stem from a need for control, but success doesn't need to follow a particular path (and some paths may be unexpected).

Conner was a senior and very anxious about his college choice. His parents were encouraging him (more strongly than they realized) to pick the same school where they met and have been active as alumni. But Conner, who had great spatial ordering but struggled with expressive language, had a feeling that their school wasn't for him. He and his parents were able to have an open discussion about his concerns and decided that he would devote a year to exploring his love of photography, including taking courses at a community college, before deciding on his future.

Watching a kid struggle is painful, and a major reason to reveal a profile is to find strategies that make schoolwork less of a struggle. However, failure does have its place in life, and fear of failure can be unwanted baggage. Whenever a student fails, in ways small or large, strive to understand in specific terms how that failure happened. What was it about the task (or problem or question or project) that might have exposed the student's neurodevelopmental weaknesses? Once you have a handle on the answer to that question, be sure to share your thinking with the student. Counterbalance failure with plenty of success; this often requires thinking creatively about sources for success, including those beyond the boundaries of schoolwork (such as leveraging affinities). Also, be on the lookout for ways to convert failure into success (such as correcting mistakes on a test to earn bonus points). Fear of failure can lead to excessive support for a struggling student, which can backfire by instilling a learned helplessness in the child. Whether you're a parent or an educator, thinking of yourself as a coach or consultant will help you guide the student toward empowerment and independence.

Tia was nine years old and her parents were at a loss as how to help her with schoolwork. They felt that everyone was jumping from idea to idea about how to support her; but pinpointing her strengths and weaknesses, with Tia's help, gave them direction. They figured out why certain academic tasks were so hard for her, which provided insight for making better choices about her instruction. As a result, they saw strategies start to work, and Tia began to experience more success.

Finally, let go of pessimism (which can be easier said than done). Kids are amazingly resilient, and you have plenty of knowledge and resources at your disposal (maybe more than you realize). Your family can make this journey, even if the course has yet to be plotted.

Things to Hold On To

So what are the key things to make sure you've packed for your journey? First, hold tight to an appreciation of the child as a unique person. Investing huge amounts of time and effort can lead to thinking about a student as a project. As a parent, make sure you have plenty of time to interact with your child outside of academic tasks. Give yourself opportunities to enjoy your child's company. If you're a teacher, take a well-rounded view of the student, and share that you have that view (such as by being tuned into the student's interests). Kids of all ages want to be liked and respected, and they can easily tell when the adults around them are focused solely on their shortcomings. In addition, avoid using labels, both clinical (such as ADHD) and nonclinical (such as "lazy" or "unmotivated"), even in your thinking.

Regularly put yourself in the child's shoes, especially when you are feeling confused or even frustrated about his school performance. Imagine what his daily experience must be like with his profile of strengths and weaknesses. School is a kid's career, so consider how you would feel if you were stuck in a job that continuously exposed your weaknesses. Getting inside the student's head not only will help you empathize but can also inspire new ideas for strategies and instructional approaches to address weaknesses and develop strengths.

Felix was sixteen and things never seemed to come easily for him at school, though everyone agreed that he was bright and charismatic. One of his teachers sat down with him to discuss his learning and Felix was able to identify what was hard and what was challenging. His teacher pledged to check in with him periodically, and they both agreed to some adjustments in his study approach and workload. By the end of the school year Felix acknowledged that work seemed a little easier, especially now that he had an ally at school.

Whether you're a parent or an educator, do what you can to normalize the situation. You naturally want to take the initiative, but do so with a sense of calm deliberation. Everybody experiences a learning challenge at some point, and the world has never ground to a halt as a result. Learning struggles should be a part of the tapestry of a family or a classroom, but it need not and should not be the dominant swatch of fabric.

For parents, part of normalizing a family environment is being mindful of what's happening with siblings. Brothers and sisters may resent what they perceive as an imbalance in time or attention in favor of a struggling learner. Explain to them what you're doing to support the struggling learner (for instance, that you're connecting a strategy, such as spending time modifying word sounds, to a neurodevelopmental function, such as phonological processing). But also find ways to continue nurturing your relationships with everyone in the family.

Sheelea couldn't wait to be a big girl so she could go to school like her older sisters. She was so excited on the first day of kindergarten. Pretty soon, though, that excitement began to wear off and it was completely gone by the end of first grade as she faced huge struggles with academics. Now seven, Sheelea's parents pushed for an explanation about her learning difficulties. Identifying her strengths and weaknesses has lit the path toward better strategies for home and school. Sheelea has also begun to understand that she's not a "dummy" and that she can be successful in school like her sisters.

Be attuned to your own needs. Part of the safety demonstration on airliners is the instruction to put an oxygen mask over your own face first (in case of depressurization) and then to put a mask on your child, because if you're overcome, your child will be in dire straits. So make time for whatever activities recharge your batteries, stimulate your thinking, enrich your knowledge, or brighten your outlook. Time is precious, but think of time spent addressing your own needs as an investment that will yield more positive results for your child. Plus, don't go it alone. Find partners to support you, such as by sharing information, serving as sounding boards for ideas, listening to you vent, or making you laugh. Admitting that you need help isn't a sign of weakness—it's a mark of wisdom.

Keep a vice grip on your appreciation of the power of strengths and affinities. Revealing the positive can make students feel so much better about themselves, especially given how defeated struggling learners can become. In the long run, a student's strengths are more important than their weaknesses. Schools have a tendency to tap a fairly narrow range of abilities and skills. But think of how many opportunities await in adulthood.

Finally, hold on to the knowledge that every learner can succeed. The picture of success is going to differ from learner to learner and from situation to situation. Success may start to come quickly, but most often it takes time and work. Struggling students rarely, if ever, reach success on their own. In most instances, they need at least one adult who is supportive, understanding, and patient. You can be that person. You can be the guide on the journey to success.

APPENDIX ONE:
PROFILE WORKSHEET

		CLUES	
		TROUBLE SIGNS	POSITIVE SIGNS
ATTENTION	Mental energy		
	Processing control		
	Production control		
MEMORY	Active working		
	Long-term storage		
	Long-term access		
LANGUAGE	Receptive		
	Expressive		
	Phonological processing		
	Semantics		
	Syntax		
	Verbal elaboration		
OTHER	Spatial ordering		
	Graphomotor function		
	Conceptual understanding		
	Applied reasoning		

APPENDIX TWO:
CASE STORY INDEX

Stories about students can help make sense of learning issues. This index includes many of the case stories described in the book. For easier reference, they are listed by grade, then by academic trouble(s), neurodevelopmental weakness(es), and neurodevelopmental strength(s).

GRADE	NAME	PAGE(S)	ACADEMIC TROUBLE(S)	NEURODEVELOPMENTAL WEAKNESS(ES)	NEURODEVELOPMENTAL STRENGTH(S)
2	Cetera	1–3, 5–8, 14, 207–208	Reading, spelling	Long-term memory	Phonological processing
2	Brady	1–8, 14, 32, 207–208	Reading, spelling	Phonological processing	Spatial ordering, receptive language, long-term memory, social cognition
3	Kal	97–98	Independent work	Conceptual understanding	-NA-
4	Tate	22	Homework	Attention processing control	-NA-
4	Finn	38–39	Math word problems	Attention processing control, syntax, semantics	Long-term memory
5	Hei	34–36	Writing	Mental energy, graphomotor function	Expressive language
6	Courtney	21–22, 96, 115	Homework, especially writing	Attention production control	-NA-
7	Monika	23, 111–112	Homework	Active working memory	-NA-

8	Ivey	47–48, 113	-NA-	Receptive language, expressive language	Spatial ordering, attention processing control, attentionl
9	Felix	16, 212–213	Study skills	Attention processing control	Long-term memory storage
9	Nabia	15–16, 25, 43	Test-taking	Long-term memory access	Long-term memory storage
10	Seung	101–102	Class discussion, conversation	Attention processing control	Expressive language
11	Rafa	98–99	Independent work	Attention processing control	Receptive language, expressive language
12	Macaria	114–115	Writing	Applied reasoning	-NA-

ACADEMIC TROUBLE(S)	NEURODEVELOPMENTAL WEAKNESS(ES)	NAME	GRADE	PAGE(S)
Class discussions and conversation	Attention processing control	Seung	10	101–102
Homework	Attention processing control	Tate	4	22
Homework	Active working memory	Monika	7	23, 111–112
Homework (especially writing)	Attention production control	Courtney	6	21–22, 96, 115
Independent work	Conceptual understanding	Kal	3	97–98
Independent work	Attention processing control	Rafa	11	98–99
Math word problems	Attention processing control, syntax, semantics	Finn	4	38–39
Reading	Long-term memory	Cetera	2	1–3, 5–8, 14, 207–208
Reading	Phonological processing	Brady	2	1–8, 14, 32, 207–208
Spelling	Long-term memory	Cetera	2	1–3, 5–8, 14, 32, 207–208
Spelling	Phonological processing	Brady	2	1–8, 14, 32, 207–208
Study skills	Attention processing control	Felix	9	16, 212–213
Test-taking	Long-term memory access	Nabia	9	15–16, 25, 43
Writing	Mental energy, graphomotor function	Hei	5	34–36
Writing	Applied reasoning	Macaria	12	114–115

NEURODEVELOPMENTAL WEAKNESS(ES)	ACADEMIC TROUBLE(S)	NAME	GRADE	PAGE(S)
Active working memory	Homework	Monika	7	23, 111–112
Applied reasoning	Writing	Macaria	12	114–115
Attention processing control	Class discussions and conversation	Seung	10	101–102
Attention processing control	Homework	Tate	4	22
Attention processing control	Independent work	Rafa	11	98–99
Attention processing control	Math word problems	Finn	4	38–39
Attention processing control	Study skills	Felix	9	212–213
Attention production control	Homework (especially writing)	Courtney	6	21–22, 96, 115
Conceptual understanding	Independent work	Kal	3	97–98
Expressive language	-NA-	Ivey	8	47–48, 113
Graphomotor function	Writing	Hei	5	34–36
Long-term memory	Reading	Cetera	2	1–3, 5–8, 14, 207–208
Long-term memory	Spelling	Cetera	2	1–3, 5–8, 14, 207–208
Long-term memory access	Test-taking	Nabia	9	15–16, 25, 43
Mental energy	Writing	Hei	5	34–36
Phonological processing	Reading	Brady	2	1–8, 14, 32, 207–208
Phonological processing	Spelling	Brady	2	1–8, 14, 32, 207–208
Receptive language	-NA-	Ivey	8	47–48, 113
Semantics	Math word problems	Finn	4	38–39
Syntax	Math word problems	Finn	4	38–39

NEURODEVELOPMENTAL STRENGTH(S)	GRADE	NAME	PAGE(S)
Attention processing control	8	Ivey	47–48, 113
Attention production control	8	Ivey	47–48, 113
Expressive language	5	Hei	34–36
Expressive language	10	Seung	101–102
Expressive language	11	Rafa	98–99
Long-term memory	2	Brady	1–8, 14, 32, 207–208
Long-term memory	4	Finn	38–39
Long-term memory memory storage	9	Felix	212–213
Long-term memory memory storage	9	Nabia	15–16, 25, 43
Phonological processing	2	Cetera	1–3, 5–8, 14, 207–208
Receptive language	2	Brady	1–8, 14, 32, 207–208
Receptive language	11	Rafa	98–99
Social cognition	2	Brady	1–8, 14, 32, 207–208
Spatial ordering	2	Brady	1–8, 14, 32, 207–208
Spatial ordering	8	Ivey	47–48, 113

APPENDIX THREE:
ATLAS OF NEURODEVELOPMENTAL
TERMS

This atlas defines the neurodevelopmental terminology cited throughout the book. Most of the terms are grouped into the categories of attention, memory, and language. Explanations, or definitions, are provided for each term, as well as some metaphors to help you understand them and describe them to students. Also provided is a description of what it feels like when the neurodevelopmental function is not reliable (everyone has these abilities, it's just that for some individuals an ability may not be dependable). Finally, the atlas includes "what to look for (and where)," which summarizes the potential clues described in Chapters One and Three. To learn more about these and other neurodevelopmental terms, read *A Mind at a Time*, by Mel Levine, or visit *www.allkindsofminds.org*.

Attention: Mental Energy

EXPLANATIONS	METAPHORS	WHAT IT FEELS LIKE IF IT'S NOT RELIABLE
The amount and reliability of cognitive fuel for staying alert and productive	Gas tank, fuel lines, miles per gallon	Mentally drained, like you have pulled an all-nighter

What to Look for (and Where)

Writing

- Excessive mental fatigue when writing
- Writing that is shorter and simpler than spoken language

Other

- Extremely pulled to nonacademic activities
- Excessive need for movement (for example, fidgeting)

Attention: Processing Control

EXPLANATIONS	METAPHORS	WHAT IT FEELS LIKE IF IT'S NOT RELIABLE
Taking in information (for schoolwork, primarily through seeing and hearing); targeting the right information (vs. distractions), absorbing information deeply enough, picking up details, maintaining focus for appropriate amounts of time	Laser beam, spotlight, magnifying glass	Mind jumping around, distracted by sights and sounds; overwhelmed by details, such as the onslaught of minutiae on tax forms; hearing or reading things but information "goes in one ear and out the other"

What to Look for (and Where)

Reading Comprehension

- Easier time comprehending when reading than when listening

Math Reasoning

- Confused by math word problems
- Misreading details in math problems (such as adding in a subtraction problem)

Information Literacy

- Trouble prioritizing search engine results
- Oversurfing on the Internet

Other

- Wandering mind
- Extremely pulled to nonacademic activities
- Particular difficulty with multiple-choice questions
- Problems sticking with a topic during conversation, or with shifting inappropriately
- Disorganized with spaces and materials
- Problems following directions
- Chronic distraction, loss of focus

Attention: Production Control

EXPLANATIONS	METAPHORS	WHAT IT FEELS LIKE IF IT'S NOT RELIABLE
Planning, resisting impulses, working at the right speed (not too fast), self-checking for accuracy and quality, incorporating feedback to make improvements	Blueprints, brakes, stoplight, speedometer, speed limit signs, dashboard	Words and actions just flow with little or no forethought; always seems to be working at full throttle, to the point that quality suffers; frequently making mistakes that easily could be avoided with more careful checking

What to Look for (and Where)

Writing (Especially Writing Process)

- Few self-corrections
- Inconsistent spelling and written mechanics
- Writing in which ideas are disorganized

Math Reasoning

- Haphazard approach to solving math problems
- Few self-corrections

Other

- Jumping into a task too quickly
- Making little, avoidable mistakes
- Particular difficulty with multiple-choice questions
- Disorganized time and thinking
- Revved up motor
- Trouble planning before starting to work, overuse of trial and error

Memory: Active Working

EXPLANATIONS	METAPHORS	WHAT IT FEELS LIKE IF IT'S NOT RELIABLE
Keeping information in mind while using or manipulating it; mentally juggling materials	A computer's RAM, counter space, juggler	Information just evaporates or slips away while thinking about it

What to Look for (and Where)

Math Procedures

- Not following math procedures accurately
- Limited capacity to perform mental math calculations

Reading Comprehension

- Forgetting information from other parts of a passage

Spelling

- Spelling accuracy better with isolated words than with words in context
- Inconsistent spelling of the same words

Writing

- Writing that is shorter and simpler than spoken language
- Inconsistent written mechanics

Other

- Getting lost in the middle of a task
- Disorganized time and thinking

Memory: Long-term Storage

EXPLANATIONS	METAPHORS	WHAT IT FEELS LIKE IF IT'S NOT RELIABLE
Placing information in memory banks, ideally in multiple mental files that are cross-referenced	Placing books on library shelves; uploading to a hard drive; putting files in a cabinet	Information rarely makes a deep mental imprint; facts seem to get filed haphazardly rather than into clear categories

What to Look for (and Where)

Math (Including Facts, Procedures, and Operations)

- Math fact recall that is inaccurate or incomplete
- Not following math procedures accurately

Phonics (Including Decoding and Spelling)

- Spelling that sounds close but looks wrong (like *laffter* for *laughter*)
- Decoding errors with irregularly spelled words (such as *answer*)
- Easier time comprehending when listening than when reading

Writing Mechanics

- Errors with writing mechanics, such as where to put commas

Information Literacy

- Not recalling how to use a search engine, including all of its features

Other

- Trouble with both recognition and open-ended questions
- Asking lots of how-to questions
- Excessive need for support (from teachers or peers)

Memory: Long-term Access

EXPLANATIONS	METAPHORS	WHAT IT FEELS LIKE IF IT'S NOT RELIABLE
Pulling information from memory banks	Pulling books from library shelves; downloading from a hard drive; getting files from a cabinet	Can't pull out information when needed without a hint or clue; information feels like it's "on the tip of the tongue"

What to Look for (and Where)

Math (Including Facts, Procedures, and Operations)

- Math fact recall that is inaccurate or incomplete
- Math fact recall that is accurate but not automatic
- Not following math procedures accurately
- Better capacity to recognize procedures than to recall them

Phonics (Including Decoding and Spelling)

- Spelling that sounds close but looks wrong (like *laffter* for *laughter*)
- Better recognition spelling than recall spelling
- Decoding errors with irregularly spelled words (such as *answer*)
- Easier time comprehending when listening than when reading

Writing Mechanics

- Errors with writing mechanics, such as where to put commas
- Easier time editing than using mechanics independently

Information Literacy

- Not recalling how to use a search engine, including all its features

Other

- Harder time with open-ended questions than with recognition questions
- Asking lots of how-to questions
- Excessive need for support (from teachers or peers)

Language: Receptive

EXPLANATIONS	METAPHORS	WHAT IT FEELS LIKE IF IT'S NOT RELIABLE
Comprehending words, sentences, and longer pieces of language, usually through listening or reading	Interpreter who listens to or reads language and makes sense of it	Words and sentences don't make much sense, as if you're in a country where you barely speak the language

What to Look for (and Where)

Reading Comprehension

- Difficulty understanding reading text
- Easier time comprehending when reading than when listening

Information Literacy

- Trouble prioritizing search engine results

Other

- Avoiding language-based leisure activities (such as reading)
- Difficulty getting what others are saying
- Confused by questions and comments
- Need for visual augmentation of verbal material
- Avoiding social interactions

Language: Expressive

EXPLANATIONS	METAPHORS	WHAT IT FEELS LIKE IF IT'S NOT RELIABLE
Communicating ideas by using words, forming sentences, and building extended pieces of language, usually through speaking or writing	Translator who takes ideas and puts them into language	Having ideas but can't quite translate them into the right words and sentences, like talking in a different language

What to Look for (and Where)

Writing (Especially Writing Process)

- Writing that is longer and clearer than spoken language
- Trouble posing and defending arguments in writing

Other

- Avoiding language-based leisure activities (such as creative writing)
- Trouble with efficiently retrieving the right words
- Avoiding social interactions
- Difficulties with behavior and conflict resolution

Language: Phonological Processing

EXPLANATIONS	METAPHORS	WHAT IT FEELS LIKE IF IT'S NOT RELIABLE
Accurately hearing the small and subtle sounds that make up spoken words; manipulating word sounds, sometimes changing words in the process; an oral process (phonics is an academic skill that connects sounds to printed letters)	Radio receiver that is sensitive enough to pick up sounds within words	Hard time distinguishing word sounds from each other (such as the four sounds in *bump*, including the /m/); words seem to be just big, single sounds or a jumble of unrecognizable sounds; word sound games, such as rhyming, don't come naturally

What to Look for (and Where)

Phonics (Including Decoding and Spelling)

- Decoding errors with regularly spelled words (such as *basket*)
- Spelling that looks close but sounds wrong (such as *laughther* for *laughter*)
- Easier time comprehending when listening than when reading

Other

- Trouble rhyming words
- Difficulty altering words by shifting sounds around (such as changing the first sound in *might* to create *tight*)

Language: Semantics

EXPLANATIONS	METAPHORS	WHAT IT FEELS LIKE IF IT'S NOT RELIABLE
Vocabulary knowledge, including understanding definitions and effectively using words	Personal dictionary or thesaurus; database of available vocabulary	Words and definitions don't connect very well; as though you're always seeing words for the very first time

What to Look for (and Where)

Reading Comprehension

- Trouble understanding words encountered in text

Writing

- Vocabulary sparse in written work

Math Reasoning

- Confused by math word problems, especially key words and terms

Other

- Narrow range of words used during conversation
- Words misused during conversation
- Difficulty making sense of explanations

Language: Syntax

EXPLANATIONS	METAPHORS	WHAT IT FEELS LIKE IF IT'S NOT RELIABLE
Understanding sentence structures (such as grammar, word order) and building sentences	Subtitles that translate dialogue from a foreign-language film; assembly line that generates finished products (sentences) from raw materials (words)	Word order in sentences is confusing; it's a struggle putting together words into clear sentences

What to Look for (and Where)

Reading Comprehension

- Confused by different sentence structures encountered in text

Writing

- Overreliance on basic sentence structures when writing

Math Reasoning

- Confused by math word problems

Other

- Overreliance on basic sentence structures when talking
- Problems following directions

Language: Verbal Elaboration

EXPLANATIONS	METAPHORS	WHAT IT FEELS LIKE IF IT'S NOT RELIABLE
Capacity to take ideas and extend them through language, using words to expand thinking	Speechwriter who takes core ideas and expands them into language	Knowing what you want to say but having a hard time explaining it so that someone else understands what you're thinking; struggling to think of another way to explain or describe something other than to repeat what you already said or wrote

What to Look for (and Where)

Writing

• Writing that does not contain extended thinking

Other

• Tendency to talk only when spoken to, use of very brief responses
• Trouble formulating elaborate responses or comments

Spatial Ordering

EXPLANATIONS	METAPHORS	WHAT IT FEELS LIKE IF IT'S NOT RELIABLE
Understanding visual information (such as a diagram) and creating material that is primarily nonverbal (such as a drawing or a model)	Camera, sketchpad	Looking at a puzzle or picture and not being able to make sense of it; being at a loss as to how to draw, fix, or construct something

What to Look for (and Where)

Math (Including Concepts, Reasoning, Procedures, and Operations)

• Confused by math visuals
• Visually disorganized math work

Writing Mechanics

• Errors with writing mechanics, such as where to put commas

Other

• Disorganized spaces and materials
• Steers clear of activities that are highly visual

Graphomotor Function

EXPLANATIONS	METAPHORS	WHAT IT FEELS LIKE IF IT'S NOT RELIABLE
Coordination of movements for handwriting	Printer and the cable connecting it to the computer	Writing with your wrist in a cast, with numbed fingers; writing with a pen that has a very slippery tip

What to Look for (and Where)

Writing

- Pencil grip that isn't tripod
- Watching pencil intently
- Heavy print
- Irregular-looking letters
- Visually disorganized writing
- Writing that is shorter and simpler than spoken language
- Unorthodox, inefficient letter formation movements

Math Reasoning and Operations

- Visually disorganized math work

Conceptual Understanding

EXPLANATIONS	METAPHORS	WHAT IT FEELS LIKE IF IT'S NOT RELIABLE
Using critical features (verbal or nonverbal) of a group of ideas or objects to define that group, determine group membership, and connect the group to other groups	Atlas that describes countries and refers to other parts of the world; Internet pages with keywords and hyperlinks	Terms seem like isolated pieces of information; hard to see connections between different objects or ideas

What to Look for (and Where)

Math (Including Concepts and Reasoning)

- Particular difficulty with applying math procedures to novel situations
- Math diagrams that are more pictorial than schematic

Information Literacy

- Picking ineffective search engine words

Other

- Asking lots of what's-up questions
- Particular trouble with thinking questions
- Difficulty making connections between related ideas and points
- Difficulty making sense of explanations
- Excessive need for support (from teachers or peers)
- Confused by questions and comments

Applied Reasoning

EXPLANATIONS	METAPHORS	WHAT IT FEELS LIKE IF IT'S NOT RELIABLE
Using logical approaches to navigate challenging situations and solve problems	A computer's central processing unit (CPU); scientist conducting experiments	Difficult to think things through; most problems seem like unsolvable mysteries or impossible puzzles

What to Look for (and Where)

Math Reasoning

- Trouble using reasoning and logic to discover a solution

Writing (Especially Writing Process)

- Trouble posing and defending arguments in writing

Information Literacy

- Picking ineffective search engine words

Other

- Asking lots of how-to questions
- Particular trouble with thinking questions
- Trouble discussing opinions or controversies

APPENDIX FOUR:
GLOSSARY OF ACADEMIC SKILLS

The following table contains terms and explanations related to academic skills. In addition, the neurodevelopmental functions involved for each skill are listed. Only the primary functions are included (the attention control systems are involved, to some extent, for just about every academic skill). Some skills involve more functions than others, with writing an example of a very complex task. Long-term memory is linked to several academic skills, reflecting its importance for schoolwork; however, long-term memory demands are not nearly as pervasive in adulthood (good news for any student struggling with long-term memory). Finally, this is not intended to be an exhaustive list of academic skills, because many other skills are necessary for success in school, such as note taking, listening comprehension, planning and executing long-term projects, and working with digital media (sometimes collaboratively). Knowing about the neurodevelopmental functions involved in skills such as reading and writing, however, paves the way to task-analyzing other skills.

TERM	EXPLANATION	PRIMARY NEURODEVELOP-MENTAL FUNCTIONS INVOLVED
Information literacy	Skill set that includes accessing (with search engines) and evaluating digital information such as that available on the Internet	Attention processing control Long-term memory access Receptive language Conceptual understanding Applied reasoning
Math concepts	Core ideas necessary for understanding math, such as equivalency (any operation performed to one side of an equation also has to be performed to the other side)	Spatial ordering Conceptual understanding
Math facts	The fundamental equivalents for math work, such as $2 + 3 = 5$, $11 - 2 = 9$, $7 \times 9 = 63$, and $32 \div 4 = 8$	Long-term memory storage Long-term memory access
Math operations	Numerical calculation skills (such as long division, simplifying a fraction, factoring an equation)	Long-term memory storage Long-term memory access Spatial ordering
Math procedures	The sequenced steps (such as for borrowing a number when subtracting) needed to perform math operations	Active working memory Long-term memory storage Long-term memory access
Math reasoning	Applying procedures, understanding concepts, and utilizing facts to solve problems, often word problems	Attention processing control Attention production control Semantics Syntax Spatial ordering Conceptual understanding Applied reasoning
Phonics	Connecting language sounds to individual letters or letter groups, such as the sound /f/ to the letters f or ph or gh (as in the word rough)	Long-term memory storage Long-term memory access Phonological processing

Reading comprehension	Understanding the meaning of printed text	Attention processing control Active working memory Receptive language Semantics Syntax
Reading decoding	Reading printed words (sometimes known as calling out words), though not necessarily understanding the words; can happen by recognizing the appearance of the word (such as a sight word) or by breaking the word apart and attacking it piece by piece and using phonics	Long-term memory storage Long-term memory access Phonological processing
Spelling	Using phonics, knowledge of common letter patterns (such as *tion*) and rules (such as "i before c. . .") to create written words	Active working memory Long-term memory storage Long-term memory access Phonological processing
Writing	Expressing ideas with printed words, either handwritten or typed; includes the use of written mechanics and a writing process	Attention mental energy Attention production control Active working memory Expressive language Semantics Syntax Verbal elaboration Graphomotor function Applied reasoning
Writing mechanics	Using rules and devices such as periods, commas, apostrophes, and quotation marks	Long-term memory storage Long-term memory access Spatial ordering
Writing process	The organization and plan used to compose written text	Attention production control Expressive language

Primary Neurodevelopmental Functions Involved in Core Academic Skills

	Attention			Memory			Language						Other			
	Mental energy	Processing Control	Production control	Active working	Long-term Storage	Long-term Access	Receptive	Expressive	Phonological Processing	Semantics	Syntax	Verbal Elaboration	Spatial Ordering	Graphomotor Function	Conceptual Understanding	Applied Reasoning
Information literacy*		X				X	X								X	X
Math concepts													X		X	
Math facts					X	X										
Math operations*				X	X	X										
Math procedures			X	X	X	X							X			
Math reasoning*		X			X	X				X	X		X		X	X
Phonics									X							

Reading comprehension*		X				X	X	X				
Reading decoding*			X	X			X			X		
Spelling*		X	X	X			X			X		
Writing*	X	X	X		X	X	X	X	X		X	X
Writing mechanics			X	X					X			
Writing process		X			X							

*Described in more detail in the tables on the following pages.

Information Literacy

ATTENTION PROCESSING CONTROL	LONG-TERM MEMORY ACCESS	RECEPTIVE LANGUAGE	CONCEPTUAL UNDERSTANDING	APPLIED REASONING
Trouble signs: Trouble prioritizing search engine results Oversurfing on the Internet	*Trouble signs:* Not recalling how to use a search engine, including all its features	*Trouble signs:* Trouble prioritizing search engine results	*Trouble signs:* Picking ineffective search engine words	*Trouble signs:* Picking ineffective search engine words

Math Operations

LONG-TERM MEMORY STORAGE	LONG-TERM MEMORY ACCESS	SPATIAL ORDERING
Trouble signs:	*Trouble signs:*	*Trouble signs:*
Math fact recall that is inaccurate or incomplete	Math fact recall that is inaccurate or incomplete	Confused by math visuals
Not following math procedures accurately	Math fact recall that is accurate but not automatic	Visually disorganized math work
	Not following math procedures accurately	
	Better capacity to recognize procedures than to recall them	

Math Reasoning

ATTENTION PROCESSING CONTROL	ATTENTION PRODUCTION CONTROL	SEMANTICS	SYNTAX	SPATIAL ORDERING	CONCEPTUAL UNDERSTANDING	APPLIED REASONING
Trouble signs: Confused by math word problem Misreading details in math problems (such as adding in a subtraction problem)	*Trouble signs:* Haphazard approach to solving math problems Few self-corrections	*Trouble signs:* Confused by math word problems, especially keywords and terms	*Trouble signs:* Confused by math word problems	*Trouble signs:* Confused by math visuals/ Visually disorganized math work	*Trouble signs:* Particular difficulty with applying math procedures to novel situations Math diagrams that are more pictorial than schematic	*Trouble signs:* Trouble using reasoning and logic to discover a solution

Reading Comprehension

ATTENTION PROCESSING CONTROL	ACTIVE WORKING MEMORY	RECEPTIVE LANGUAGE	SEMANTICS	SYNTAX
Trouble signs: Easier time comprehending when reading than when listening	*Trouble signs:* Forgetting information from other parts of a passage	*Trouble signs:* Difficulty understanding reading text Easier time comprehending when reading than when listening	*Trouble signs:* Trouble understanding words encountered in text	*Trouble signs:* Confused by different sentence structures encountered in text

Reading Decoding

LONG-TERM MEMORY STORAGE	LONG-TERM MEMORY ACCESS	PHONOLOGICAL PROCESSING
Trouble signs:	*Trouble signs:*	*Trouble signs:*
Easier time comprehending when listening than when reading	Easier time comprehending when listening than when reading	Easier time comprehending when listening than when reading
Decoding errors with irregularly spelled words (such as *answer*)	Decoding errors with irregularly spelled words (such as *answer*)	Decoding errors with regularly spelled words (such as *basket*)

Spelling

ACTIVE WORKING MEMORY	LONG-TERM MEMORY STORAGE	LONG-TERM MEMORY ACCESS	PHONOLOGICAL PROCESSING
Trouble signs: Spelling accuracy better with isolated words than with words in context	*Trouble signs:* Easier time comprehending when listening than when reading	*Trouble signs:* Easier time comprehending when listening than when reading	*Trouble signs:* Easier time comprehending when listening than when reading
Inconsistent spelling of the same words	Spelling that sounds close but looks wrong (like *laffter* for *laughter*)	Spelling that sounds close but looks wrong (like *laffter* for *laughter*)	Spelling that looks close but sounds wrong (such as *laughther* for *laughter*)
		Better recognition spelling than recall spelling	

Writing

ATTENTION MENTAL ENERGY	ATTENTION PRODUCTION CONTROL	ACTIVE WORKING MEMORY	EXPRESSIVE LANGUAGE	SEMANTICS	SYNTAX	VERBAL ELABORATION	GRAPHOMOTOR FUNCTION	APPLIED REASONING
Trouble signs: Excessive mental fatigue when writing	*Trouble signs:* Few self-corrections	*Trouble signs:* Writing that is shorter and simpler than spoken language	*Trouble signs:* Writing that is longer and clearer than spoken language	*Trouble signs:* Vocabulary sparse in written work	*Trouble signs:* Overreliance on basic sentence structures when writing	*Trouble signs:* Writing that does not contain extended thinking	*Trouble signs:* Pencil grip that isn't tripod	*Trouble signs:* Trouble posing and defending arguments in writing
Writing that is shorter and simpler than spoken language	Inconsistent spelling and written mechanics	Inconsistent written mechanics	Trouble posing and defending arguments in writing				Watching pencil intently	
	Writing that is disorganized in terms of ideas						Heavy print	
							Irregular-looking letters	
							Visually disorganized writing	
							Writing that is shorter and simpler than spoken language	
							Unorthodox, inefficient letter-formation movements	

Note: Writing mechanics also utilizes long-term memory and spatial ordering, especially for such things as punctuation rules that are often memorized in terms of how writing should look on the page (for instance, how commas and quotation marks are arranged).

APPENDIX FIVE:
GLOSSARY OF TESTING TERMS

This glossary can help you be a better customer of learning assessments. It contains several terms that have not been mentioned in the book but that you may encounter during the assessment process (such as during a school meeting or in a written report).

TERM	EXPLANATION
battery	Many tests consist of several *subtests*, which collectively may be referred to as a *battery*. In addition, a learning assessment may incorporate many types of tests, which also may be called a *battery*.
bell curve	Most tests, when administered to enough students, reveal a particular pattern when plotted on a graph with scores on the horizontal *x*-axis and number of students on the vertical *y*-axis; most students' scores fall at or around the mean score and tail off at the high and low ends of the score range. The resulting shape (and expected pattern of scores that produce it) is often referred to as the bell curve.
confidence interval	Any test samples a student's knowledge and skills, so a test score is just an estimate of knowledge or skill level. The *confidence interval* is the range around a student's score, usually expressed in ± score points, that is likely to contain the actual score that equates to skill or ability level. In general, a narrow interval (such as 110 ± 3) reflects greater *reliability* than a broader interval (such as 110 ± 7).
discrepancy formula	Also known as the discrepancy model, this is the practice of subtracting a student's standardized achievement scores from his *IQ* score. Since the early 1970s, this has been the dominant way of determining a student's eligibility for special education services for a learning disability (the standard generally has been a difference of 15 or more points between IQ and achievement scores). This practice has been criticized on several grounds, and new federal regulations no longer require public schools to use it (although it has not been banned); *response to intervention* (RTI) is now an alternative for determining special education eligibility.
factor	Many tests are actually a collection of several *subtests*, and sometimes *subtests* with important similarities are grouped together. Such a grouping is often called a *factor*, and it can have its own *standard score*. For example, all of the *subtests* that display material to the student to memorize might be grouped into the "Visual Memory" factor.
IQ	This is the commonly known acronym for *intelligence quotient*. The original idea was to divide a student's test score by the

average score for his age to get a quotient that was then multiplied by 100, so any score above 100 suggested above-average intelligence. Contemporary *intelligence tests* compute IQ differently, by taking the points a student earns on the test and comparing the student's performance to that of same-age students on a scale that usually puts 100 right in the middle. A strong performance (or a lot of points earned) results in an IQ score that is above 100. So an IQ score is essentially a way to compare one student to a group of same-age students (see *standard score*).

intelligence test
This is a measure (usually administered to an individual student) of intelligence, an umbrella term for many brain-based abilities such as reasoning, language use, abstract thinking, and problem solving. Several theories exist that differ in their claims about the specific contents and organization of intelligence; many intelligence tests are designed according to a particular theory. Almost all such tests are collections of *subtests*, and many also include *factors*.

long form
A test's full set of *subtests* and resulting score(s) is its *long form* and provides a broader view of what the student can do than a *short form* of the test.

percentile
This is a *standard score* with a range of 0 to 100, with 50 representing average performance. A strong performance (or a lot of test points earned) results in a *percentile* that is above 50. If a student gets a *percentile* of 67, then his performance is as strong as or better than 67 percent of other students the same age who also took the test.

reliability
The consistency of a test to measure abilities or skills is referred to as its *reliability*. If you step on a bathroom scale three times and get the same weight (or very close to it) each time, then the scale has good *reliability*. A test first has to be reliable before it can be said to really measure what it is intended to measure (see *validity*). Two important indicators of a test's quality are *reliability* and *validity*.

response to intervention
Often referred to as RTI, this is an approach to identifying students who have learning problems and for determining the type and extent of instruction they receive in school; identification is usually based on curriculum-specific probes that measure using local norms (that is, comparing a student to peers in the class or school). For many years, determining eligibility for special education for a learning disability was based on the difference between a student's *IQ* and standardized achievement test results (see *discrepancy formula*). Recent changes to federal law opened the

door for RTI, which is becoming increasingly widespread. RTI is especially well-suited for discreet skill areas, such as decoding, but questions remain about how to apply it to the upper grades and with more complex work, such as term papers and projects.

RTI	See *response to intervention*.
score, grade level	A *standard score* that compares a student's test performance to the grade levels of other students who took the same test is a *grade-level score*. A strong performance (or a lot of test points earned) results in a *grade-level score* that is above the student's current grade level.
score, scaled	This is a *standard score*, usually with a range of 1 to 19, with 10 representing average performance. Most subtests provide *scaled scores*. A strong performance (or a lot of test points earned) results in a *scaled score* that is above 10. If a student gets a *scaled score* of 13, his performance is better than most other students the same age who also took the test.
score, standard	A *standard score* is computed by taking the points a student earns on a test or *subtest* and comparing them to the performance of same-age students; the scale may vary (see *IQ, grade level score, percentile, scaled score, subtest score, T score*, and *z score*). In essence, *standard score* compares one student to a group of same-age students.
score, subtest	This is a *standard score*, usually a *scaled score* with a range of 1 to 19, which represents how well a student performed on a *subtest*. On *intelligence tests*, the *IQ* is usually a composite of several *subtest scores*.
score, T	A *standard score* with a range of 10 to 90 with 50 representing average performance is a *T score*. A strong performance (or a lot of test points earned) results in a *T score* that is above 50. If a student gets a *T score* of 60, then his performance is better than that of most other students the same age who also took the test.
score, z	This is a *standard score* with a range of −4 to +4, with 0 representing average performance. A strong performance (or a lot of test points earned) results in a *z score* that is positive, or above 0. If a student gets a *z score* of +1, his performance is better than most other students the same age who also took the test.
short form	Some tests, such as *intelligence tests*, may provide the option of only using some of the *subtests* and then getting a score based on just those *subtests*. The reason for such a *short form* is to have a faster way to sample a student's abilities or skills. Obviously the downside is that a narrower perspective is taken on what the student can do than with the *long form* of the test.

standardized   When a test (or *subtest*) is designed to be administered with prescribed procedures (for consistency from student to student), it is said to be *standardized*. Such tests provide *standard scores*, which compare a student's performance to that of same-age peers.

subtest   Most standardized tests, such as *intelligence tests*, consist of several discrete tasks, each of which generates its own *standard score*.

validity   The extent to which a test measures what it is intended to measure is its *validity*. If you step on four different bathroom scales and get the same weight (or very close to it) each time, but then step on a fifth scale and get a much different weight, that scale probably has weak *validity*. Two important indicators of a test's quality are *validity* and *reliability*.

INDEX

A

Academic skills, referral questions based on, 175–176
Access practice, 134
Active reading tactics, 128
Active working memory, 22–23, 28, 36, 105–106, 175–176, 195, 226–227; and direction-following games, 71–72; limited capacity, 54–55; and math procedures, 226; and memory gaps, 73; and reading comprehension, 227; referral questions based on, 178; and spelling, 227; and spelling in isolation, 110; and student interactions, 107; work samples, 118–119; and writing, 227
Activity choice, 108–109
Affinities, 194; leveraging, 58–59, 79
All Kinds of Minds (www. allkindsofminds.org), 8, 92; training from, 157
Applied reasoning, 28, 44, 52, 177, 236–237; example expert referral question, 166; and information literacy, 237; and math reasoning, 236; referral questions based on, 179; work samples, 119; and writing, 237
Assessments, *See* Learning assessments
Atlas of Neurodevelopmental Terms, 17, 19, 27, 85, 147, 195, 223–238; active

working memory, 226–227; applied reasoning, 236–237; conceptual understanding, 235–236; expressive language, 230–231; graphomotor function, 235; long-term memory access/storage, 227–229; mental energy, 224; phonological processing, 231–232; processing control, 224–225; production control, 225–226; receptive language, 230; semantics, 232; spatial ordering, 234; syntax, 233; verbal elaboration, 233–234
Attention, 29, 175, 176; example expert referral question, 166; games, creating, 65; home strategies, 61–66; mental energy, 23, 28, 66, 100, 129–130, 224; modeling for your child, 61; organization systems, 61–62; processing control, 16, 28–29, 53, 66, 100, 106, 224–225; production control, 54, 225–226; reward systems, 63–64; as set of brain functions, 21; sports/ extracurricular activities, 65–66; work schedules, 62–63; *See also* Unreliable attention

B

Basis for comparison, finding, 15
Battery, 252
Behavior, and language problems, 109

Revealing Minds

Assessing to Understand and Support
Struggling Learners

By: **CRAIG POHLMAN**

ISBN: 978-0-7879-8790-9
Paperback

Revealing Minds is a hands-on guide for assessing learning problems in school-aged students, based on the philosophy of the cutting-edge institute All Kinds of Minds. The book presents a unique approach that stresses the importance of identifying a student's assets and uncovering breakdown points that lead to problems in school. It is filled with real-life examples, definitions of key terms, diagrams, and sample assessment tasks.

"Any clinician, advocate, parent, or educator who wants to truly understand and help children who struggle in school should read this book and will want to return to it often." —**Paul B. Yellin**, M.D., FAAP, Director, Yellin Center for Student Success and Associate Professor of Pediatrics, New York University School of Medicine

"Pohlman provides us with a cogent, step-by-step guide to conducting assessments." —**Katherine Balisterri Howard**, M.A., NCSP, school psychologist, Old Trail School, Bath, Ohio

"Draws the essential connections between theory and practice that can enable every teacher to be 'smart' about assessing student learning—not just of those who struggle, but all students." —**Peter Gow**, Director of College Counseling and Special Programs, Beaver Country Day School

"This book is unique in presenting a clearly defined, respectful, and practical approach to assessing learning differences in children." —**Elizabeth Briere**, M.D., FAAP, Executive Director, Center for Student Success